DAWN
THROUGH OUR
DARKNESS

Prayers and Reflections

Compiled by
GILES HARCOURT

Collins

Collins Liturgical Publications
8 Grafton Street, London W1X 3LA

Distributed in USA by
Harper & Row, Publishers, Inc., San Francisco
Icehouse One — 401
151 Union Street, San Francisco, CA 94111-1299

Distributed in Canada by
Novalis, Box 9700, Terminal,
375 Rideau St, Ottawa, Ontario K1G 4B4

Distributed in Ireland by
Educational Company of Ireland
21 Talbot Street, Dublin 1

Collins Liturgical Australia
PO Box 316, Blackburn, Victoria 3130

Collins Liturgical New Zealand
PO Box 1, Auckland

ISBN 0 00 599842 5

First published 1985
Third printing 1987
© compilation Giles Harcourt 1985

Cover photo by J. L. Law
Typographical design by Colin Reed
Made and printed in Great Britain by
Bell & Bain Ltd, Glasgow

DAWN
THROUGH OUR
DARKNESS

Dawn may be called the opening of the light.
Dawn may be called the closing of the dark.
It is the start of day or end of night.
It is a death-and-birth dividing mark.
At dawn a world is just about to be.

John Fandel

Foreword

Prayer, we are told, is 'the lifting up of the mind and heart to God'. Some people need very little in the way of helps to prayer; others a good deal. But we all have, in varying degrees, a deep-felt need for that communication with God.

Giles Harcourt offers a selection of texts — aphorisms, thoughts, scripture quotations, prayers —to help us to pray. His texts and quotations cover a great many circumstances — blessings and joys, crosses and troubles — of daily life.

A wise Abbot of Downside, Father John Chapman, once gave this advice: *Pray as you can, not as you can't*. Much more important than methods and techniques is simply to open ourselves to God. 'Do not worry about having few words or nothing to say. The fewer the words the more chance of listening for God to speak', Giles Harcourt tells us. This too is good advice, and I am sure that the present book will help many people in our troubled and uneasy times 'to hear what the Lord God has to say, a voice that speaks of peace'.

VICTOR FARWELL OSB
Abbot of Worth

Acknowledgements

The publishers are grateful for permission to reproduce the following copyright material:

New English Bible, Oxford and Cambridge University Press © 1970.

Various prayers and Collects, some adapted, from *The Alternative Service Book 1980*, © Central Board of Church Finance, Church of England.

Reform Synagogues of Great Britain, for prayers from *Forms of Prayer for Jewish Worship, Daily and Sabbath*, © 1977.

Roger Bush, *Prayers for Pagans*, Hodder and Stoughton, London 1968. Used by permission of Curtis Brown (Aust) Pty. Ltd. Sydney.

Dylan Thomas, *The Poems*, J.M. Dent. Used by permission of David Higham Associates Ltd.

Michel Quoist, Gill and Macmillan.

Margaret Evening, *Who Walks Alone*, Hodder and Stoughton Ltd.

The Methodist Marriage Service, Methodist Publishing House.
The Methodist Service Book, Methodist Publishing House.
The Methodist Covenant Service, Methodist Publishing House.
Methodist Revision, Methodist Publishing House.

Doris Stickney, *Water Bugs and Dragonflies*, © 1982 The Pilgrim Press. Used by permission of A.R. Mowbray & Co. Ltd.

Laurie Lee, *I Can't Stay Long*, Penguin Books 1975. Used by permission of Andre Deutsch.

R.H. Lloyd, *Assemblies for School and Children's Church*, Pergamon Press, pp. 2-3. Used by permission of Religious and Moral Education Press.

Bishop John Taylor, *Go Between God*, SCM Press.

T.S. Eliot, from *Collected Poems 1909-1962*, Faber & Faber Ltd, Publishers.

W.H. Auden, 'New Year Letter', *Collected Poems*, Faber and Faber Ltd.

Dag Hammarskjold, *Markings*, (translated by W.H. Auden and Leif Sjöberg), Faber and Faber Ltd.

Note

Every effort has been made to identify the sources of these prayers, which have been collected over many years. Where it has not been possible to trace sources, the publishers would be grateful for any additional information from readers. **Items not ascribed to others are by the compiler.**

Introduction

This book is a sharing of a journey, from the first seeds of anxiety and doubt into the dark earth of crisis and despair, to break through into the fresh light of acceptance and understanding.

Many people today feel as though they are buried, even suffocated, in darkness.

Yet darkness is not necessarily threatening; night may be the time for rest and growing, the prelude to deeper truths and fresh discoveries. At the heart of the Christian faith are cross and resurrection – darkness before light. The way to conquer the powers of darkness is not to run away, for then our fears become our shadows. Rather we are to confront the darkness of our fears and trials with the light which is Christ. In this way Christ becomes dawn through our darkness.

No matter which faith we hold or whether we have none, all of us need a way of life, a philosophy, a set of values which point the way and sustain us in times of difficulty, temptation or crisis. We also need to be reminded, in a materialistic and claustrophobic age, that there is a dimension of our lives which is more fulfilling than just see, feel, grab and discard.

Peace for our lives depends not on what we have but on what we essentially are, spiritual beings, God's own. To know and love and share God is his purpose intended for our delight, and prayer is the language of the heart that gives us access to God.

We need therefore to pray so that no opportunity is lost for our replenishment. Prayer then is the great restorative.

HOW SHALL WE PRAY?
The answer is simply and sincerely, as to a very good friend. First relax, and don't feel you have to speak. Take time to catch your breath and settle. With friends, you do not have to rush; neither do you with God.

It is not until we are quiet and still within ourselves that we are totally ready to pray. This can be anywhere at any time – at home, in the street, while travelling, at work, at leisure, when moving or being still. Stillness though is preferable, for then you are not so distracted. Planes *can* refuel in the air, but normally they refuel on the ground.

To help you to be still, try and find a hard-backed chair in a quiet place, or lie flat on the floor, or stand upright. I have found a straight back (unless you have physical problems) essential. Then slow steady breathing. Closing your eyes may help you concentrate. But if you are unable to concentrate in this way then focus on something peaceful – a person, a plant, a lighted candle, a picture or an aspect of beauty or silence. Think *only* about that. Hold to this for two to three minutes and you will become alert and relaxed, aware of thought without bodily sensation. Do not do anything yet. Just *listen*. Notice in the listening, first the sounds far away . . . then the sounds nearby . . . and finally the sounds within yourself (all part of God's creation, his creation for our appreciation).

In letting yourself be calmed you are beginning the first lesson of trust, allowing yourself to wait upon another and be dependent upon the other to supply a need. You are also beginning the first step in training yourself to *concentrate*. The will, for this purpose, is more important than the feelings.

Do not worry about wandering thoughts. Do not worry about what to pray; that will come. Concentrate on being still, silent, open, alert, listening.

Now you are ready to pray.

WHAT SHALL WE PRAY?
Here are some suggestions.

Start by stopping! Stop to be thankful for all you have already been given without even asking. Think of all the people and things for which you are truly thankful. Name them (and *out loud* if it helps to centre this reality). When you are delighted give thanks with joy. Praise God for the things that warm your heart. And through making such comparison, acknowledging such generosity, we are made to reflect on how ungenerous and insensitive we have been. Admit therefore where you have injured or marred God's creation, and failed to appreciate and honour his gifts. Confess your sorrow. Ask his forgiveness.

Then pray for others, that his nearness, strength, comfort and support will uphold them. Never try to manipulate prayers for selfish ends, for that is to play God. If we pray before we act he will enable us to be open and sensitively alert to the needs of others.

Now, for the first time ask what is spiritually necessary for yourself. Then conclude with thanksgiving, and with the Lord's Prayer and the Grace (see later).

Some people find that if they are in a hurry or a crisis, short 'arrow prayers' are helpful. Others like to repeat a sentence or a phrase. Whatever your method the important need is to pray, regularly and whenever you can.

It is decidedly helpful to have a rule as to when you pray. Like exercise, better a little each day than a lot once in a while. Start with a daily minimum of 5 minutes and build up from there. If we are honest we could all benefit from at least 15 minutes' quiet-time each day; the busier or more isolated we become the greater our need. Many people find that the early morning and half an hour in the early evening, when work or the main activity of the day is over, are real oases of peace and strengthening, which give not only energy but quality to the next part of the day. Similarly, if you are denied work or creativity, two portions of peace and quiet are important stabilisers during an often purposeless day. If you start and end each day with thanksgiving you will come to discern a new order of priorities and understanding, whatever your circumstances. This, in turn, will feed the rest of the day or night, heal divisions within you, and help to release that which is locked away in your life.

Like a small pebble thrown into a pond, the tiny seed planted in a large field, or the solitary lighthouse in great and turbulent darkness, each of these images is in its different way a pattern for prayer that can begin for us and others a great and strengthening influence.

This book is a collection of prayers and meditations that are the fruit of praying in the way I have suggested. You can think of them as companions to your own praying; sometimes they will comfort you, at other times they will inspire you.

It is therefore hoped that this book will encourage a renewing process, and at whichever level of need, what we begin in prayer will eventually draw us from personal darkness to greater nearness with God, who is the source of all our light and joy.

Giles Harcourt

ABANDONED (alone)

Lord, you have taught us in your Son
that real love begins
where nothing is expected in return.
Help us to journey into the desert
that we may learn again
the simplicity of true values,
the power of a strengthened spirit, and
the peace that comes
from being close to you.
May we follow you each day
in all self-denial and tenderness of soul.   Amen.

ABORTION

A million seconds in loving
A thousand hours in feeding
A hundred hopes in giving
A day and night in waiting
An afternoon in hospital
A minute for excision
A second to end a life
And now, Lord,
I ache
from this minute, this day, this year, this life,
ache in heart and soul
for there is no life in me . . .
Yet, Lord, there is you . . . always you.   Amen.

Lord, I feel terrible
and in the darkness of this ending
all alone,
though others surround my bed.
In the darkness of noon
your son felt the same
though others surrounded his head.
How Lord do thorns and friends
darkness and despair

become a message of hope?
Even though this moment
seems more intense and more real
than any other,
help me to understand
that the pains of Calvary
are not ever
Easter Day.   Amen.

It does not matter now *why*, Lord. Whether danger or
illness or disease or irresponsibility. This abortion is
the end of possibility, the fading out of hope, of lives
being enriched and blessings given.
    Help me, Lord, in my pain and suffering as you
helped your son; and as you strengthen me, help me to
understand and to value deeply and sincerely the gift of
life in you, through Jesus Christ our Lord.   Amen.

ACCUSATION

You who are 17
blame me because
the world is in a mess.

When I was 17
we talked about
the Treaty of Versailles

And so we pass
the buck right back to Adam;
so let me

Ask in the name of
my small son,
aged 3

About insecticide,
the colour bar,
the H bomb
and the pill.

You will be 31
when he is 17.
What (if anything)

Will you have done
to dodge the accusation
of my son?

Sydney Carter

ACTIONS

Like father like son — your actions show whose
spiritual sons you are.
  Dorothy L. Sayers 1893–1957, The Man Born to be King

Decide who and what you want to be; then pursue
your purpose with total concentration until you become
what you wish to be.

In our actions, we should accord with the will of
heaven.

Chinese aphorism

When you do a favour, do not expect a reward.
Chinese aphorism

Whenever you do a thing, act so that it will give your
friends no occasion for regret and your foes no cause
for joy.

Chinese aphorism

ADDICTS

Lord I am an addict and I need help, now.
  Help me to seek help swiftly. Help me to listen
carefully, think fairly and accept humbly.
  Even though I may be desperate, let those who help
see my true need, and in the spirit of your son, do
what is helpful, loving and necessary,
immediately.   Amen.

ADOPTION (mother's prayer)

I turn to you in awe because you have put your trust in me. I bless you for the love which binds me to my child; and for the wonder of creation which you have renewed within my heart.

AGGRESSION

No man will confide in one who shows himself as aggressive. And he whom no man confides in will remain solitary and without support.

Lieh Tzu

Lord, my aggression is like a whirlwind catching me up in its power. I become volcanic, insistent, consuming. All now! Lord, thank you for such energy, such wonderful potential. Teach me how to reflect on the consequences of my intentions before I act. Teach me to channel my energies to your will in stages. Teach me, Lord, teach me . . . to honour your gift.   Amen.

AGING

My deafness I endure.
To dentures I'm resigned.
Bifocals I can manage
But God how I miss my mind.

Anonymous

Aging is not a problem to be solved. It is an opportunity. Parishes are rich with the experience, expertise, wisdom and faith of older people. We must discover ways to seize this gracious gift as a blessing.

The Episcopalian *(USA) May 1984 (adapted)*

The arrogance of age must submit to be taught by youth.

Eamund Burke 1729–1797

To love playthings well as a child, to lead an adventurous and honourable youth, and to settle when the time arrives, into a green and smiling age, is to be a good artist in life and deserve well of yourself and your neighbour.

Robert Louis Stevenson 1850–1894

A man that is young in years may be old in hours.

Sir Francis Bacon 1561–1626

How to know you are growing older

Everything hurts and what doesn't hurt, doesn't work.

The gleam in your eye is from the sun hitting your bifocals.

You feel like the night before, and you haven't been anywhere.

Your little black book contains only names ending in M.D.

You get winded playing chess.

Your children begin to look middle aged.

You finally reach the top of the ladder and find it leaning against the wrong wall.

You join a health club and don't go.

You begin to outlive enthusiasm.

Your mind makes commitments your body can't meet.

You know all the answers, but nobody asks you the questions.

You look forward to a dull evening.

You walk with your head held high trying to get used to your bifocals.

You turn out the light for economic rather than romantic reasons.

You sit in the rocking chair and can't get it going.

Your knees buckle and your belt won't.

You regret all those mistakes resisting temptation.

You're 17 around the neck, 42 round the waist, and 106 round the golf course.

You stop looking forward to your next birthday.

Dialling long distance wears you out.
You're startled the first time you are addressed as
  old-timer.
You remember today, that yesterday was your
  wedding anniversary.
You just can't stand people who are intolerant.
The best part of the day is over when the alarm
  clock goes off.
Your back goes out more than you do.
A fortune-teller offers to read your face.
Your pacemaker makes the garage door go up
  when you watch a pretty girl go by.
You sink your teeth into a steak and they stay
  there.
You get exercise acting as a pallbearer for your
  friends who exercise.
You get too much room in the house and not
  enough in the medicine cabinet.
The little grey-haired lady you help across the
  street is your wife.

Anonymous

AGNOSTICS

I remember, Lord, and am very humbled when I look at
you, that I will always be agnostic about some things,
and at some time agnostic about others. Thank you for
giving me time in which to learn that not all things are
to be revealed at once, and truths are often learnt
sharply or gradually.   Amen.

AIM

No great achievement is possible without persistent
  work.

Bertrand Russell 1872–1970

My God, make known to me what
I must now do to please you, for
I desire to do without reserve
whatever you require of me.

St Alphonso Di Liguori 1696–1787

Eternal father, you alone can control
the days that are gone
and the deeds that are done.
Remove from my burdened memory
the weight of past years.
Set free from the clamour of complacency
and the palsy of remorse,
let me reach forward
to what is before me
and press on toward the goal
of your high calling in Jesus Christ.

Bishop Charles Henry Brent 1862–1929 (adapted)

Make me useful, positive, appreciative, generous.
Make me live.

Norman Goodacre, Layman's Lent

Catch, then, O catch the transient hour
Improve each moment as it flies.
Life's a brief summer, man a flower
He dies, alas, how soon he dies.

Samuel Johnson 1709–1784

Resolve to be thyself: and know, that he
who finds himself, loses his memory.

Matthew Arnold 1822–1888

First, never go against the best light you have;
secondly, take care that your light be not darkness.

Matthew Arnold 1822–1888

To know the world, not to love her, is thy point;
She gives but little, nor that little, long.

Edward Young 1683–1765

To begin with oneself, but not to end with oneself;
To start from oneself, but not to aim at oneself;
To comprehend oneself, but not to be preoccupied with
oneself.

Martin Buber 1878–1965

In saying 'I know who I am' Don Quixote
said only: 'I know what I will be', that is
the hinge of all human life: to know
what one wills to be.
Little ought you to care who you are;
the urgent thing is what you will to be.

And your longing impulse toward the one
you will to be is only homesickness
drawing you toward your divine home.
Man is complete and upstanding only
when he would be more than man.
Miguel de Unamuno 1864–1936

Store what you must:
Share what you can.

Work for peace within your household,
then in your street,
then in your town.
Bershider Rebbe, d. 1816

Challenge the will to summon energies.
Assault small-mindedness.
Lift people out of loneliness to fellowship.
Make war on doubt until souls
Spread truth.
Remember to be gentle.
Tubby Clayton 1885–1972

AIMLESS (or lost or in despair)
Find yourself a teacher, get yourself a friend.
Joshua Ben Perachyah, 2nd century BC

Do not separate yourself from the community.
Do not trust in yourself till the day of your death.
Do not judge your fellow man until you have been in
his position.
Hillel, 1st century

ALARM (bell continually ringing)

That alarm bell keeps on and on, Lord; it's driving me crazy. Stop it! stop it! stop it! stop it! What can I do? I shut the door; I close the windows, draw the curtains and muffle my ears, but still it goes on. Penetrating.

Thank you, Lord, for telling me in this muffled irritation to put on some classical music and pray into this noise, this situation; pray for those who are nearer than I to the noise and cannot protect their ears; pray for those who may come to silence the noise; pray for the imperfect there, and in me, to be perfected.

For if a mechanism can do that in its inflexibility, what do I do who have so much time and movement at my disposal?

Lord teach me to reverence sound, and remember those who cannot hear anything.   Amen.

ALONE

How am I to face the odds
of man's bedevilment and God's?
I, a stranger and afraid
In a world I never made.

A. E. Housman 1859–1936

The enlightened man is watchful over himself even when alone.

AMBITION

Unnumber'd suppliants crowd Preferment's gate,
Athirst for wealth, and burning to be great;
Delusive Fortune hears the incessant call.
They mount, they shine, evaporate and fall.

Samuel Johnson 1709–1784

ALCOHOLICS

The twelve steps of alcoholics anonymous

1 We admitted we were powerless over alcohol,* that our lives had become unmanageable.
2 Came to believe that a power greater than ourselves could restore us to sanity.
3 Made a decision to turn our will and our lives over to the care of God as we understood him.
4 Made a searching and fearless moral inventory of ourselves.
5 Admitted to God, to ourselves, and to another human being the exact nature of our wrongs.
6 Were entirely ready to have God remove all these defects of character.
7 Humbly asked him to remove our shortcomings.
8 Made a list of all persons we had harmed, and became willing to make amends to them all.
9 Made direct amends to such people wherever possible, except when to do so would injure them or others.
10 Continued to take personal inventory and when we were wrong promptly admitted it.
11 Sought through prayer and meditation to improve our conscious contact with God as we understood him, praying only for knowledge of his will for us and the power to carry that out.
12 Having had a spiritual awakening as the result of those steps we tried to carry this message to alcoholics and to practise these principles in all our affairs.

Alcoholics Anonymous Fellowship,
Twelve Steps and Twelve Traditions, *1953*

* or any other compulsive symptom

O God, give me the sincerity to accept the things I cannot change, the courage to change the things I can, and the wisdom to know the difference.

Rheinhold Niebuhr 1892–1971

AMPUTATION

Lord, I hate you with a deep loathing. You are cutting part of me off. Me whom you say you love. How could you! How dare you! You did it to your son. Now you are doing it to me. What is the matter with you? Don't you ever learn?

Well, if you are so damned smart come along with me into my pain and suffering, my fear and anger. You did it for your son. Now do it for me. Please. Amen.

Help me to understand, Lord, that loss of this part of my body is not an end to life, your great gift to us all. Removal of some of my strength and ability can give me more need of you, and more of your strength for sharing with others.

ANAESTHETICS

Anaesthetics are a testing of trust, Lord. But my faith is in you.

Give to those who administer anaesthetics great care and true skill, that by eye and hand they may be gentle and understanding.

Give to me the trust in your power to use the darkness for curing, and to use the recovery for renewed awareness of confidence in you. Amen.

ANGER

To hide such a feeling is to increase its force a thousand times.

Chinese aphorism

I was angry with my friend:
I told my wrath, my wrath did end.
I was angry with my foe
I told it not, my wrath did grow.

William Blake 1757–1827, 'A Poison Tree'

ANGELUS, The

The angel of the Lord brought tidings to Mary:
and she conceived by the Holy Spirit.

Hail Mary, full of grace, the Lord is with thee; blessed
art thou among women, and blessed is the fruit of thy
womb Jesus. Holy Mary, Mother of God, pray for us
sinners, now, and at the hour of our death.   Amen.

Behold the handmaid of the Lord:
be it unto me according to thy word.

Hail Mary, etc.

And the Word was made flesh:
and dwelt among us.

Hail Mary, etc.

Pray for us, O holy Mother of God:
that we may be made worthy of the promises of Christ.

We beseech thee O Lord, pour thy grace into our
hearts; that as we have known the incarnation of thy
son Jesus Christ by the message of an angel, so by his
cross and passion we may be brought to the glory of
his resurrection. Through the same Christ our
Lord.   Amen.

ANIMALS

Lord, help us to remember
that in loving animals
we love you,
that in loving animals
we see aspects
of your kindness,
your devotion,
your love.
In their kindness
can be our healing.
In their devotion
can be our reassurance.
In their love
can be our joy.

Dear Lord
Let me try
to love
the fly.

Dog

My blessed dog, no one knows what you meant to me,
and of you they have said, 'It was only a dog!' Is it
foolish that my eyes grow dim when I think of you,
and life seems all empty without you, and still more is
it futile for me to believe that there is a place where
you will go to where there is happiness for you and
some reward for your gallantry, your faithfulness, and
your unquestioning love? . . . If I were God, there
would be green fields in which you should run, and
endless bones which you could retrieve, and though —
forgive me — I could give you no cats to chase, I would
give you such happy days, such peaceful sleep, and at
least the power to dream that you were out hunting in
the woods.

Dick Sheppard 1880–1937

Humour

When God had finished the stars and whirl of coloured
    suns
He turned his mind from big things to fashion little
    ones;
Beautiful tiny things (like daisies) he made, and then
He made the comical ones in case the minds of men
Should stiffen and become
Dull, humourless and glum
And so forgetful of their maker be
As to take even themselves — *quite seriously.*
Caterpillars and cats are lively and excellent puns:
All God's jokes are good — even the practical ones!
And as for the duck, I think God must have smiled a
    bit
Seeing those bright eyes blink on the day he fashioned
    it.
And he's probably laughing still at the sound that came
    out of its bill!

F. W. Harvey

Cruelty

O Lord, who hates nothing that you have made, keep us from all cruelty to animals, birds or any of your creatures. May we always remember that you have made both them and us, and show them the mercy that we have received from you; for your name's sake.   Amen.

ANOINTING, Sacrament of (Holy Unction)

The sacrament of anointing is a sacrament of affirmation. It ranges from peace for the dying, and strengthening for the perplexed, the sick or the afraid, to God's rejoicing in new life, restoration and wholeness. Births, baptisms, marriages, and mended quarrels, family reunions and anniversaries, moments of delight, thankfulness and joy can be sacramentally blessed through anointing.

Ask for anointing; consult your minister or priest.

Prayers of anointing

1 *Priest:*	Out of his great love for you may the Lord calm your mind and imbue your spirit with his peace, that as you are eased from all burdens and cleansed from all worries you may perceive deep within your soul the supreme power which he alone can give. For by this most holy anointing is the nearness of his presence and power to endure pain and fear, sorrow and despair that slowly but surely you may be drawn from your darkness into his marvellous light, which confers light, and peace.
Recipient:	Amen.
2 *Priest:*	Through this holy anointing and his great love for you, the Lord fill you with the power of the Holy Spirit.
Recipient:	Amen.

Prayers of anointing (ctd)

3 *Priest:* In the name of the most high God and in his infinite love and power, may freedom from all sickness and infirmity of body, mind and spirit be granted to you, through Jesus Christ our Lord.

Recipient: Amen.

4 *Priest:* In the name of our Lord Jesus Christ, may the healing power of his most holy Spirit anoint you afresh this day in your inmost being, working in you his perfect gift of healing.

Recipient: Amen.

5 *Priest:* In the name of Jesus of Nazareth feel and know deep within yourself the power of his redemptive love and the innermost healing of your soul, so that despair gives way to hope, and enlightenment to peace, touched and confirmed by the eternal power of his love.

Recipient: Amen.

6 *Priest:* In the name of Jesus of Nazareth, the one name under heaven by whom and through whom we may be saved, and brought to a knowledge of the truth, in his name we lay our hands upon you. May he give you his peace, in heart and mind, and strength sufficient for all your needs in and through which you may serve him and glorify his holy name, and the blessing of God Almighty, the Father, the Son, and the Holy Spirit be with you now and always.

Recipient: Amen.

Reginald Barnard

ANOTHER

Whatever happens to oneself happens to another.

Oscar Wilde 1854–1900

ANXIETY

Take no thought for the morrow. Is not the soul more than meat? Is not the body more than clothing?

Matthew 6:25

The Lord is near; have no anxiety, but in everything make your requests known to God in prayer and petition with thanksgiving. Then the peace of God, which is beyond our utmost understanding, will keep guard over your hearts and your thoughts, in Christ Jesus.

Philippians 4:6–7, New English Bible

Lord, for this I pray
that in this paradox
of tension and relief
of privilege and denial
of love and hatred
you may create heaven.

Ugandan prayer

Teach me, Lord, not to be anxious when I have done what you have given me to do; help me my Saviour, to leave the issue to your wisdom.   Amen.

Bishop Brooke Foss Westcott 1825–1901 (adapted)

APATHY

I suffer from Acedia, spiritual drought, torpor of the soul. I have periods of utter weariness, when life does not mean anything at all, and everything goes grey.

Han Suyin

Lord, help me to raise my eyes and look for possibilities. The flight of the bird, the growth of the flower; all show the way. Let me trust in you to awaken me.   Amen.

What is spiritual apathy? It means to have the standard changed by leaving out the ideals, it means to have the standard changed to correspond with what we who now live in this place actually are. But when the price of becoming a Christian is so cheap, then comes idleness, and then comes doubt, why Christianity need be. And that is perfectly true; for if the requirement is no greater, then a saviour, a redeemer, grace etc, become fantastic luxuries. What Christianity presupposes, namely, the tortures of a contrite conscience, the need of grace, the deeply felt need, all these frightful inward conflicts and sufferings — what Christianity presupposes in order to introduce and apply grace, salvation, the hope of eternal blessedness — all this is not to be found, or is to be found only in burlesque abridgement — at bottom it is sheer superfluity which at the most one imagines the need of. And so in the end one becomes tired of Christianity; for the pressure of imitation was lacking, the ideal, Christ as Pattern.

Sören Kierkegaard 1813–1855

APOLOGY

A man should never be ashamed to own that he has been in the wrong, which is saying in other words that he is wiser today than he was yesterday.

Alexander Pope 1688–1744

APPRECIATION

One of the deepest needs of the human heart is the need to be appreciated. Every human being craves to be accepted for what he is ... when I am not accepted, then something in me is broken ... When a person is loved for what he *is*, then he becomes a unique and irreplaceable personality ... Each of us longs to find in life some other person to whom we can really talk, and with whom we can share our lives honestly, and openly — someone who will understand us and accept us completely. God is that person.

Peter Van Breemen, As Bread that is Broken

ASCENSION, The

Father, we thank you that the truth of the Ascension of your blessed son is that he is not only living but Lord over all creation.

This most tremendous truth makes powerful claims not only for you, but also on us.

You are indeed sovereign of all, even over those mysterious forces which appear to have us in their grip. For you are in control even when we are not.

Your call, through the guidance of the most holy Spirit, is in all things to be obedient to you, so that all may be fulfilled, through Jesus Christ our Lord.   Amen.

ASSURANCE

I have made you a little like myself.
I have given you a mind to know what is good.
I have given you a heart to love what is good.
I have given you a will to do things that make other
    people happy.

Sirach 17:1f

ATHEISTS

Lord, I know that those who deny your existence have yet to prove that that is true. But I am more interested in those atheists who are hardened in heart being opened to the wisdom and love of your spirit. And those who are kind, but refuse to acknowledge you, being held in that kindness and deepened in love, for that is the way of your son, Jesus Christ, my Lord, through whose love you give me the power to share my life with them.   Amen.

See also Death

ATTITUDE

Hear no evil
see no evil
speak no evil.

Anonymous

Listen
observe
keep a confidence
and a trust
and be cheerful.

We live partly in a world of fact and partly in a world
of value; but the values must always control the facts.
Dean Inge 1860–1954

My soul is athirst for God, yea even for the living God.
Put thy trust in God.

Psalm 42:2

Hold no man insignificant.

Ben Azzai, 2nd century

Be first to greet every man.
Rabbi Mattitya Ben Heresh, 2nd century

Love be in my head
and in my understanding.

Love be in my eyes
and in my looking.

Love be in my mouth
and in my speaking.

Love be in my heart
and in my thinking.

Love be in my end
and at my departing.

Sarum Missal (adapted)

Pay attention to the state of your soul.

Anonymous

The mind is its own place, and in itself
can make a heaven of hell, a hell of heaven.
John Milton 1608–1674

AUTUMN

Coldly, sadly descends
The autumn evening. The field
Strewn with its dark yellow drifts
Of wither'd leaves, and the elms,
Fade into dimness apace,
Silent.

Matthew Arnold 1822–1888, 'Rugby Chapel'

AUXILIARY HELP

Lord, pour the blessing of your love on all who exercise
the care and patience of auxiliary help. Give them kind
words, warm hearts, willing hands and silence when
needed, through him who is infinitely caring, Jesus
Christ our Lord.   Amen.

AWARENESS

Self-awareness

Let us ask Christ to make us more and more sensitive
to the richness and fulness of life, that dwelling in him
we may see its beauty as he sees it. Let us thank him,

For the joy of movement, of music and song,
For the beauty of form and colour and fragrance,
For all the earth's loveliness in field and flower and
    tree,
For the love and companionship of friends,
For the adventure of thinking and working together,
For fun and laughter which deepen understanding,
For these, and for so many other gifts,

We thank you O Lord.

Awareness of others

We remember those who are cut off from many of the
joys of life or whose vision of its purpose is empty and
spoiled — the blind and deaf, the crippled and
disabled, those who have become embittered by
grinding toil and poverty, by cruelty and wrong, all

whose lives are lonely and cheerless.

O God, whose great and tender love is over all your
children, we pray for those for whom life is darkened
by ill-health, poverty, or lack of work; for all whose
minds are distressed, for whom faith and hope seem
dead. May your fatherly hand be upon them and your
great comfort about them. May they in all their grief
and distress have the comfort of your support; and, O
Lord, show me if there is any way in which I may help
to bear their burden.   Amen.

BAPTISMAL VOWS, Reaffirming of

This most frequently takes place when Christians
welcome new Christians in holy baptism.

However it increasingly takes place at confirmation
services and during Holy Week or at Easter, when all
say together:

I turn to Christ
I repent of my sins
I renounce evil
I believe and trust in him.

BATH

Evening

Lord, a shower is for washing, a basin for quick
cleaning, but a bath is for resting, stretching and being
warmly at ease.

Thank you Lord for the benison of hot water that
soothes away cares; for the smooth kindliness of soap
and the heaven of unburdening the day.   Amen.

Morning

Dear Father and eternal spirit, as your blessed son came
to the Jordan so that all righteousness could be fulfilled,
let the warmth and cleansing of this water imbue me
with your love, your zeal and your peace to go out into
the world, joyfully.   Amen.

BAPTISM, Sacrament of

Baptism is the sacrament which gives entry into the Christian community. The promises made at the baptism service are for a deep commitment in return for a great gift (bought at a great price). They are expected to be taken seriously. In an age of divided families and broken relationships, the Church, as the community of Christ's followers, is here to help integrate lives and whole families into the warmth of Christian love.

Love cannot be given or shared in isolation. A parent or child who never sees the family is no more than a nominal member. The same is true of the Christian family. Sharing, caring, laughing, worship and expressing thankfulness, are best done together.

Rivers enable water to flow. Roads enable traffic to reach its destination. Sacraments are channels for enabling God's power to flow into and direct our lives. The sacrament of baptism is the outward sign by which God, in his great love for us, calls us to be his own. In receiving this sacrament we become his and part of life eternal. In his giving us this sacrament our lives are enhanced by his strength and guidance uniquely revealed through Jesus Christ. As with Christ and his disciples we become part of a fellowship which shows us how to be grateful for what we have been given, and how to share what we have. That thankfulness and sharing is done through a life-of-sharing in the community of those who love in this particular way. Through this sign, we are saved from the consequences of living only for ourselves.

At baptism we promise that we or our children will live and grow up in this un-self-centred context. We cannot grow as Christians unless we honestly try to love our fellow Christians and neighbours, and receive instruction from the Church in how we can grow as Christians. A child, teenager, or adult has to be part of the Christian community if he or she is to receive the

Baptism, Sacrament of (ctd)
insights of sharing, tolerance, kindness, understanding,
compassion and forgiveness which the loving Christian
community can give.

The sharing community or Church is a collection of
people in any area who stand by the values of Christ
which they have tested against experience and
therefore believe to be important. They say, in effect,
our first allegiance is to God through the on-going life
and example of Jesus Christ; we admit that we need
help in living; and we also need the support and
encouragement of the sharing community.

Of course you can believe in God outside the
Christian community; the Jews, Muslims, Hindus and
others do so devoutly. But for the insights of Christian
understanding you have to live in a Christian context
— not only for what you can receive but also for what
you can share and encourage for the benefit of all.

It is because the beauty and strength of Christ's
promises touch the deepest roots in our lives that we
should take the sacrament of baptism sincerely as well
as with joy.

BEAUTY

Beauty is God's handwriting — a wayside sacrament.
Welcome it in every fair face, in every fair sky, in every
flower, and thank God for it.

Ralph Waldo Emerson 1803–1882

BED

Bed, bed, that heaven upon earth to the weary head.
Thomas Hood 1799–1845

Lord, as I lie here, help me to appreciate the gift of
quietness and the powers of stillness for healing my
body and calming my soul.

Patience is never born of a hurry, and reflection is an
opportunity to think carefully and well. So let this time

be my gratitude to you for making me still, and letting me think quietly, constructively, with a generous and loving spirit.

And in the gift of sleep let my trust be in you that as guardian of my soul you will guide me and keep me safe, that asleep I may rest in peace and awake I may feel renewed, through Jesus Christ our Lord.   Amen.

BENEDICTUS

Blessed be the Lord God of Israel, for he hath visited and redeemed his people;

And hath raised up a mighty salvation for us, in the house of his servant David;

As he spake by the mouth of his holy prophets, which have been since the world began;

That we should be saved from our enemies, and from the hands of all that hate us;

To perform the mercy promised to our forefathers, and to remember his holy covenant;

To perform the oath which he sware to our forefather Abraham, that he would give us;

That we being delivered out of the hands of our enemies might serve him without fear;

In holiness and righteousness before him all the days of our life.

And thou, child, shalt be called the prophet of the highest, for thou shalt go before the face of the Lord to prepare his ways;

To give knowledge of salvation unto his people for the remission of their sins,

Through the tender mercy of our God, whereby the dayspring from on high hath visited us;

To give light to them that sit in darkness, and in the shadow of death, and to guide our feet into the way of peace.

Luke 1:68-79

BEING

> Man has real existence, but it has nothing to do with place.
>
> *Chuang Tzu b. 369BC*

> The kingdom is a spirit-like thing, and cannot be achieved by active doing.
>
> *Lao Tze b. 604BC*

> There is nothing that says we have to be born. Merely to be alive is the great gift. All else is perks.

> You become what you admire.
>
> *Mahatma Gandhi 1868–1948*

BIRTH

> Every child comes into the world with the message that God does not despair of man.
>
> *Rabindranath Tagore 1861–1941*

> O holy child of Bethlehem
>   descend to us, we pray;
> Cast out our sin, and enter in;
>   be born in us today.
>
> *Bishop Phillips Brooks 1835–1893*

> A ray of hope flickers in the sky,
> a tiny star lights up way up high
> all across the land
> dawns a brand new morn'
> this comes to pass
> WHEN A CHILD IS BORN.
>
> *Fred Jay*

> They were all looking for a king
>   To slay their foes and lift them high;
> Thou cam'st, a little baby thing
>   That made a woman cry.
>
> *George Macdonald 1824–1905*

Our birth is but a sleep and a forgetting:
  The soul that rises with us, our life's star
Hath had elsewhere its setting
  And cometh from afar;
Not in entire forgetfulness
And not in utter nakedness,
But trailing clouds of glory do we come
  From God who is our home.

William Wordsworth 1770–1850, 'Ode. Intimations of
Immortality'

In my beginning is my end.

T. S. Eliot 1888–1965, 'East Coker'

In the beauty of the lilies Christ was born, across the
  sea,
With a glory in his bosom that transfigures you and
  me;
As he died to make men holy, let us live to make men
  free!

Julia Ward Howe 1819–1910 (and others)

Child of later years

She was born in the autumn and was a late fall in my
life, and lay purple and dented like a little bruised
plum, as though she'd been lightly trodden in the grass
and forgotten.

Then the nurse lifted her up and she came suddenly
alive, her bent legs kicking crabwise, and her first
living gesture was a thin wringing of the hands
accompanied by a far-out Hebridean lament.

This moment of meeting seemed to be a birthtime for
both of us; her first and my second life. Nothing, I
knew, would be the same again, and I think I was
reasonably shaken. I peered intently at her, looking for
familiar signs, but she was convulsed as an Aztec idol.
Was this really my daughter, this purple concentration
of anguish, this blind and protesting dwarf?

Then they handed her to me, stiff and howling, and I

held her for the first time and kissed her, and she went still and quiet as though by instinctive guile, and I was instantly enslaved by her flattery of my powers.

Only a few brief weeks have passed since that day, but already I've felt all the obvious astonishments. New-born, of course, she looked already a centenarian, tottering on the brink of an old crone's grave, exhausted, shrunken, bald as Voltaire, mopping, mowing, and twisting wrinkled claws in speechless spasms of querulous doom.

But with each day of survival she has grown younger and fatter, her face filling, drawing on life, every breath of real air healing the birth-death stain she had worn so witheringly at the beginning.

Now this girl, my child, this parcel of will and warmth fills the cottage with her obsessive purpose. The rhythmic tides of her sleeping and feeding spaciously measure the days and nights. Her frail self-absorption is a commanding presence, her helplessness strong as a rock, so that I find myself listening even to her silences as though some great engine was purring upstairs.

When awake, and not feeding, she snorts and gobbles, dryly, like a ruminative jackdaw, or strains and groans and waves her hands about as though casting invisible nets.

When I watch her at this I see her hauling in life, groping fiercely with every limb and muscle, working blind at a task no one can properly share, in a darkness where she is still alone.

She is of course just an ordinary miracle, but is also the particular late wonder of my life.

Laurie Lee, I Can't Stay Long

Stillborn

Great preparation and care has been given for the coming of this child. Great love and hope for his (her) arrival and his (her) life.

That he (she) should come into the world stillborn is to move from the hidden world before to the unrevealed beyond, to discard a stage between darkness and darkness.

To be stillborn seems a terrible denial of him (her) and of us, of potential unfulfilled, hope shattered and love cast out.

Yet your only son came to conquer death and to show us the way beyond darkness to eternal life.

Give to us, Lord, who are in a darkness deeper than the womb, the true vision of your light, your strength and your saving grace, through Jesus Christ our Lord.   Amen.

The souls of the just are in the hand of God, and no torment shall touch them. In the eyes of the foolish they appear to be dead; their departure was reckoned as defeat, and their going from us as disaster. But they are at peace, for though in the sight of men they may be punished, they have a sure hope of immortality.

Wisdom of Solomon 3:1 New English Bible (adapted)

Father, in the freedom of your creation, you allow all possibilities. For reasons we do not always know, only a part of your plan is begun within our understanding. But we believe that as sovereign of all, you have the power to save and redeem eternally. We ask you, most merciful Father, to receive *N* and fill him (her) with life everlasting, so that in the fullness of time, we who mourn bitterly and ache in sorrow, may be with him (her) and you in everlasting peace and joy, through Jesus Christ our Lord.   Amen.

For the mother and the father

Lord, so little time was given before he (she) was taken. So much love was being offered, with no hope of being received. Now he (she) is taken far away. Coming in sorrow to you, Father, surround *N* and *N* in that eternal love which surpasses the love that enfolded this still-born child in the womb, and let them know that a time is here for healing, for trust, and holding fast to you, through Jesus Christ our Lord.   Amen.

Father in heaven, we come to you as your children;

We come in sorrow that *N* has been taken from us so soon; but also we come in peace, for your son has promised that all your little ones shall look upon your loving face for ever.

We come to you in prayer for his (her) parents (mother), who have (has) so little time to care for him (her). We thank you for their (her) love, which surrounded him (her) as he (she) grew, and for your love for us all, that gives us strength.

Father, we thank you that you have created all things and made us in your own image;

That after we had fallen into sin you did not leave us in darkness, but sent your only son Jesus Christ to be our saviour;

That by his death and resurrection he broke the power of evil;

And that by sending the Holy Spirit you have made us a new creation.

We thank you that *N* is, with us, an heir of all your promises, sharer with us in the humanity that you redeemed in Christ, and in the eternal life which you have revealed to us through him.

We welcome our brother (sister) *N* into the flock of Christ in the name of the Father and of the Son and of the Holy Spirit.   Amen.

Methodist Revision

BIRTHDAY

I thank thee, Lord, for the gift of life.
There is nothing that says I have to be:
I thank thee, Lord, for the gifts of today,
But most especially for being with thee.

Lord make me wiser every year
    and better every day.

Charles Lamb 1775–1834

BITTERNESS

How much bitterness there is at the bottom of all
sweetness, or what degree of despair is hidden under
abnegation, what hatred is mingled with love.

Marguerite Yourcenar, Memoirs of Hadrian

BLESSINGS

NB   Blessings should (if possible) never be administered or
received in a hurry. Wherever possible let silence, a prayer
and preparation accompany the blessing. A blessing should
confer affirmation, love and peace. The gift of silence or
simply holding a hand, may be in itself a blessing.

The peace of God which passes all understanding keep
(y)our hearts and minds in the knowledge and love of
God, and of his Son Jesus Christ our Lord; and the +
blessing of God Almighty, the Father, the Son and the
Holy Spirit be with us (you) all evermore.   Amen.

Unto God's gracious mercy and protection we commit
    you.
The Lord + bless you and keep you,
The Lord make his face to shine upon you and be
    gracious unto you,
The Lord lift up the light of his countenance upon you
    and give you his peace,
Both now and evermore.

Numbers 6:24-26 (adapted)

Love one another with a pure heart fervently.

1 Peter 1:22

May God bless you with all that is good
And deliver you from every evil.
May he clarify your mind to understand life
And permit you to experience eternity
And there turn to you his loving face
For your happiness for ever.

Manual of Discipline

The great Spirit gives me this form
this toil in manhood
this repose in old age
this rest in death.
Surely that which is such a kind
arbiter of my life
is the best arbiter of my death.

Lord, guide, strengthen and protect all on or beneath
land, sea, and in the air or beyond.
  Be near to all in difficult and dangerous work. All
whose skill benefits others. All who seek to champion
the wronged and the oppressed, the overburdened and
the unappreciated, those who are outcast, degraded or
alone.
  Let your light be their light, your love their love, and
your peace their blessing, for Christ's sake.   Amen.

May God in his infinite love
Bless you with the grace of form,
    charity, goodness, and wisdom,
    the grace of true words and trust, and
    the grace of whole-souled loveliness
So that you may be bathed
in the showers of his light,
Your soul freed with the hands of his love,
As you wait and listen
In the beauty of his silence,
And the blessing + . . .

The Invocation of the Graces (adapted)

Thanks be to God
for all the warm blessings
of the sun.

God the creator
God the sustainer
God the redeemer
bless you now and always.

Anonymous

Share your blessings.

As you become the joy of all joyous things
Like beams of light to the sun
So may God open the doors of your hearts
That you become instruments of warmth and welcome;
and the blessing + . . .

May the light of the Lord be in your eyes
The love of the Lord be in your heart
The gentleness of the Lord be in your hands
The kindness of the Lord in all you do
And the blessing . . .

As seconds are best to minutes,
As minutes are best to hours,
Hours to days, and days to years,
So are we best to the Lord.

May the loving kindness of the Most High and his holy
protection be with you in sickness and in sorrow, in
suffering and in danger, in darkness and in light and
every hour of your need.   Amen.

May the love of the Lord Jesus draw us to himself; may
the power of the Lord Jesus strengthen us in his
service; may the joy of the Lord Jesus fill our souls; and
may the blessing of God Almighty, the Father, the Son,
and the Holy Spirit, be with you and abide with you
always.

Archbishop William Temple 1881–1944 (adapted)

May the Lord of his great mercy bless you,
  and give you understanding of his wisdom and
  grace;
May he nourish you with the riches of the Catholic
  faith, and make you to persevere in all good works;
May he keep your steps from wandering, and
  direct you into the paths of love and peace;
And the blessing of God Almighty, the Father, the Son,
  and the Holy Spirit, be upon you and remain with
  you always.

Southwark Diocese

Live in a sacred and happy manner;
Respect all life.

The grace of our Lord Jesus Christ
and the love of God
and the fellowship of the Holy Spirit
be with us all evermore.   Amen.

Entering

May God bless you as you enter every room.

Leaving

May God bless you as you go from here.

For food

Bless O Lord the hands that prepared this beautiful
meal, and those whose thankful hands receive it, for
Jesus Christ's sake.   Amen.

Farewells

God's gift is
man moving to life
from darkness to light
partial to whole
and faith into love.

Go forth into the world in peace;
Be of good courage;
Hold fast to that which is good;
Render to no one evil for evil;
Strengthen the faint-hearted;
Support the weak;
Recover the fallen;
Help the afflicted;
Honour all men;
Love and serve the Lord, rejoicing in the power of the
    Holy Spirit.
And the + blessing of God Almighty, Father, Son and
    Holy Spirit be upon you
And remain with you always.   Amen.

Anonymous

Into thy hands, O Lord
I commend my spirit
For thou hast redeemed me
O Lord thou God of truth.

Compline

The gift becomes a journeying when man is
co-operating in the divine gift.

God be with you till we meet again.

Anonymous

Goodnight

Welcome

Goodbye = God be with you.

Christmas

May you have the gladness of Christmas which is hope,
the spirit of Christmas which is peace,
the heart of Christmas which is love.

John Redmayne

BLINDNESS

Never assume because a man has no eyes he cannot see.

Chinese aphorism

BOASTING

The braggart is seldom loyal,
the glib talker seldom honest.

Chinese aphorism

BOREDOM

The dread dropsy grows by indulging itself.

Horace 65–8BC

If you are idle be not solitary; if you are solitary be not idle.

Samuel Johnson 1709–1784

He is not only dull in himself, but the cause of dullness in others.

Samuel Foote 1720–1777, cf Henry IV, Part 2 II, ii, 7

Lord if I am bored or boring it means that I need sufficient rest, sufficient filling, sufficient sharing, sufficient order and dedication to be giving rather than just waiting to receive. Fill me with your love, your puposes, your joy, and stir my foolish heart.   Amen.

BROTHER

Jealousy

And the father said to the elder brother, son, you are always with me, and all that I have is yours. It was right that we should make merry and be glad, for your brother was dead and is alive again, and was lost and is found.

Luke 15:31-32

Support
Brother clasps the hand of brother
Stepping fearless through the night.

B. S. Ingemann 1789–1862, tr. S. Baring-Gould

BURNS

Lord, in the searing pain of these burns, I remember
your agony in the heat and hottest hours of the day.

I know that you came to that terrible ordeal already
half flailed and lashed to death. Your whole body, from
head to foot, spoke of what pain can be endured.

But even greater than all these were the terrible
taunts, the savage injustice, the fading hope, the full
knowledge of being forsaken by father and friends.

And only you in your great power could bear such
terrible weakness, such unremitting pain, such
continual pain to mind, body and soul.

Be with me, Lord, and give me your strength to
endure. Be with me Lord, be with me.   Amen.

To neck and shoulder

Here now upon my
bed I lie as narthex
is to sanctuary
my body straight
my head awry.
As wooden rail
defines
the earth and
heavenly sphere (and
may be done away)
so collarbone is bare
and flesh is gone
and all I have is God
to look upon.

Sheila Mayo

CALLIPERS

The gifts of science can be the gifts of strengthening.
Thank you Lord for the men and women whose
pioneer work made these callipers possible, and help
me in their use to know and feel the strength of your
love through inventors that care.   Amen

CARING

Cast all your care on him, for he cares for you.

1 Peter 5:7

For the countryside

Take nothing but photographs.
Leave nothing but footprints.
Kill nothing but time.

A notice at Coaley Point near Stroud

CHANGE

We trained hard but it seemed that every time we were
beginning to form up into teams we would be
reorganised . . . I was to learn later in life that we tend
to meet any new situation by reorganising; and a
wonderful method it can be for creating the illusion of
progress while producing confusion, inefficiency and
demoralisation.

Petronius Arbiter 210BC

CHARACTER

By looking at a man's faults, you know the man's
character.

Confucius (K'ung Fu-tze) 551-479BC

To reveal his character, test a man when he is tired.

Listen to a man's words and look at the pupil of his
eye. How then can a man conceal his character?

Mencius (Meng K'o) 372–289BC

Tell me your companions, and I will tell you what you are.

St John Chrysostom 347–407

Judge a great man by watching what he does in little things.

Chen Chiju 1558–1639

CHATTERING

I chatter, chatter, as I flow
  To join the brimming river,
For men may come and men may go
  But I go on for ever.

Alfred, Lord Tennyson 1809–1892

Avoid godless chatter, for it will lead people into more and more ungodliness, and their talk will eat its way like gangrene.

2 Timothy 2:16, Revised Standard Version

On the telephone

The person in the call-box was in the habit of calling, any person, any time, for as long as tolerance would allow. Every evening. Hurricanes could come. People could bang. Faces become even desperate. But like the Mississippi she would just keep rolling along, oblivious of the outside world. Too bad she missed the man with the gift who called at her door. Too bad she prevented the ambulance coming in time for the sick child. Too bad she never listened to others and shared the real needs around her. Too bad, Lord, too bad.

CHILDREN

Do not threaten a child. Either punish or forgive him.

Semachot

A child should always say what's true,
And speak when he is spoken to,
And behave mannerly at table;
At least as far as he is able.

Robert Louis Stevenson 1850–1894

Children, obey your parents in all things, for this is well pleasing to the Lord. Fathers do not provoke your children, lest they should become discouraged.

Colossians 4:20-21

Discipline your children while they are young enough to learn. If you don't, you are helping them to destroy themselves.

Proverbs 19:18

Judgement

A child's judgement is only the judgement of a child. And though there be accuracy and even stinging truth, there is neither the experience nor the wisdom of years to complete the judgement by tempering it with mercy and self-understanding.

Appreciation of mother

It wasn't until John was about twelve years old that he really became self-conscious about his mother's hands. Although she was in every other way a beautiful woman, her hands were terribly scarred and twisted.

John's father was the first to notice that John, who had once brought his friends home to play, now no longer did so.

'Perhaps you would like to know how your mother came to have such hands', said his father, 'because when I married her they were lovely. One day when you were just able to toddle about, your mother turned her back for a moment. You made for the fireplace and stood too close. You screamed, and because there was nothing else available and the flames were growing, she smothered the fire with her own hands. She saved you but sacrificed her hands in doing so.'

John just looked ahead and said nothing. Soon, John once again began bringing his friends around to the house for a game or to tea. He always made a point of asking his friends very discreetly to note his mother's hands. 'You see,' he would say, 'she burnt them because she loved me so much.'

R. H. Lloyd, Assemblies for School Children's Church

Appreciation of father

I can never forget looking into the face of my father when life had left the dear body, and thinking of the times unnumbered when I failed to tell him what I owed him. They tell me that when I was young he and my mother went without things to give me of the best. I know that the thoughts of his last years were centred around me. I wonder now if there is an angel who can take him a message that will tell him that as the years go by I am increasingly grateful to him. On the last Sunday of his life he expected me to have supper with him, and told my mother several times that he was certain I should come. I was tired and did not go. That is a thing that haunts now it is too late.

Dick Sheppard 1880–1937

An intercession for all children

We come before thee, the father of all mankind, who
    didst make man in thine own image:
        Hear us we beseech thee.
That we may remember at all times that the children of
    all nations are thy children:
        Hear us we beseech thee.
That we may have and keep a sense of brotherhood
    with children in every part of the world:
        Hear us we beseech thee.
For children who have not received a fair share of the
    world's goods:

> We pray for thy blessing, O God.
For those who are sick or suffering:
> We pray for thy blessing , O God.
For men and women of all lands who have the care of
children at heart:
> We pray for thy blessing, O God.
That we may never fail to show a spirit of brotherly
love in all our dealings with people:
> Hear us we beseech thee.
For each one of us, members of thy great family:
> We pray for thy blessing, O God.   Amen.

The School Service

Play

Child's play is the nearest thing to contemplation in its
total absorption and delight.

CHRISTIANITY

Christianity is a symphony not a solo.

CHRISTIANS

A Christian is not a man who is trying to *do*
something, he is a man who has *received* something; a
man to whom something has happened and who
simply cannot keep it to himself.

Peter Marshall 1903–1949

CHRISTMAS

The Annunciation	Lord I hear Christmas is coming again; help me truly to understand what Christ's coming means.
The Journey	Lord be of help to all travelling along difficult roads, all who are in difficulty, delayed, lost or abandoned.
The Arrival	Lord let me help those who are tired and harassed especially after a long journey.
The Need	Lord, help me to recognise you in others' needs, especially the cold, hungry, the forsaken, the unattractive, the lonely and the forlorn.
The Birth	Lord let the coming of this new day give newness of meaning and worth to my life by giving up my minutes and hours to your service.
The Worship	Lord let me meet with my fellow worshippers to honour and adore your holy name and to give joyful thanks for the unique and unexpected gift of your blessed Son. Amen.

The light comes into our world

The way is long, let us go together
The way is difficult, let us help each other
The way is joyful, let us share it
The way opens before us, let us begin.

We follow the star, the light, till we are led to where he is. Then he will lead us through the wilderness and desert, the green pastures and sunlit uplands of life to, yes, crucifixion with the pain and rejection of the world, until we arrive at the gates of resurrection. But first we must follow the light till we are over the place the young child's heart will be.

This is my crisis at Christmas, Lord. It is others who conceive pleasure and are full of joy. Theirs is the safe delivery of parcels, the joy of gifts, the remembering of love, the delight, the thanks, the glitter and the glory.

I am shut out, excluded, cold and alone, just bundled
    about from door to door. . . And then
Lord, I remember . . . you were too.
Lord, you are on my side after all . . .
Lord, you are there with me in the cold, in the night, in
    the joylessness of being alone without hope or
    friends.
You are here with me . . . now . . . So please, cross your
    light with my life.   Amen.

Christmas Day

For Christ's sake, let us not forget him whose birthday
    it is.
Amidst the busyness of preparing meals,
Amidst the excitement of wrapping parcels,
Amidst the carols, the laughter, the fun,
    May the surprise of Bethlehem,
    May the simplicity of Nazareth,
    May the mature, considered expression of his love
        be real to us all who share this day.
So let this day, from dawn till darkness, bring us to
    Christ, alive for evermore, joy and gladness, too. And
    glory to your name.

                         Rita Snowden, Prayer for the Family

The nativity

Love came down at Christmas
Love all lovely, love divine
Love was born at Christmas
Stars and angels gave the sign

Not a gooey mindless love blinded to fault but a searing love which searches for truth — an enabling love which widens our horizons.

Lord help us to witness here to a love which sears through sham and show and burns with a light of truth and warmth.

Love came down at Christmas

Lord we remember that love was born at Christmas — so was the slaughter of the innocents.

We pray for all the areas of our world where innocent people are slaughtered daily; where children have been incarcerated for three years for fear of being shot; where the inhumanity of man commits atrocities in your name — the Prince of Peace — and wherever people live in fear.

Love came down at Christmas
Love all lovely . . .

Lord, life is not all lovely.

Tonight there are people who are alone and fearful. Some who feel let down and betrayed by friends or loved ones. Some who feel very sick in mind or body or who watch a loved one in such a state. Some who mourn the loss of a friend and much loved person. Lord help them to understand your love is their token.

Love shall be our token
Love be yours and love be mine
Love to God and all men
Love for plea and gift and sign

Lord, many people are searching for signs and we your Church often cloud these signs in our attempt to take you to them instead of allowing you to take us.

Tonight Lord in the stillness and the beauty of this

place come into our hearts with a renewed light and
strength so that love will be to God and all men.

Lesley Harcourt

CITY

God of the city, God of the tenement and the houses of
the rich, God of the subway and the night club, God of
the cathedral and the streets, God of the sober and the
drunk, the junkie and the stripper, the gambler and the
good family man; dear God, help us to see the world
and its children through your eyes, and to love
accordingly.

Monica Furlong

Seek the peace of the city to which I have carried you,
and pray to the Lord for it. For on its peace your own
peace depends.

Jeremiah 29:7, Forms of Prayer for Jewish Worship

This is my city, Lord
   I've flown over it
      Driven round it
         Walked through it
           and I love it.
Its concrete chasms, its quiet parks . . .
   Its massive buildings and its tiny homes.
      Its suburbs, rich and poor.
But most of all, Lord, its people . . .
   My city, Lord. Your city,
Remember, Lord, there was one city
   over which you stood and wept.
Do you weep over this city?
   With its hunger, its greed, its cruelty,
Its foolishness and heartbreak.
   Lord, I believe you do.
      For sometimes I too lie awake at night
   And listen to the agony of God,
      Your people's cry.   Amen.

Roger Bush, Prayers for Pagans (abridged)

CLOTHES

Lord, let your light be only for the day,
And darkness for the night.
And let my dress, my poor humble dress
Lie quietly over my chair at night.

Nachum Bomze 1906–1954

COLD

There is a cold, Lord, more chilling than the ice or
snow, more numbing than the dampest room. It is the
cold of indifference and the apathy that spurns all
interest. Lord give your warmth, your light and your
love to all the cold areas of the human heart.   Amen.

COLD, Having a

Lord, I am blocked in ears and nose and throat. I feel
terrible and ache. Help me in my weakness and misery.
Give me the wisdom not to infect others needlessly, but
to rest, to sleep, and to let your healing powers
proceed.   Amen.

COLLECTS

Strengthening: Advent 1

Almighty God, give us grace to cast away the works of
darkness and to put on the armour of light, now in the
time of this mortal life, in which your son Jesus Christ
came to us in great humility: so that on the last day,
when he shall come again in his glorious majesty to
judge the living and the dead, we may rise to the life
immortal; through him who is alive and reigns with
you and the Holy Spirit, one God, now and for
ever.   Amen.

Reassurance: Christmas 1

Almighty God, who wonderfully created us in your

own image and yet more wonderfully restored us
through your son Jesus Christ: grant that, as he came to
share in our humanity, so we may share the life of his
divinity; who is alive and reigns with you and the
Holy Spirit one God, now and for ever.   Amen.

Inspiration: Epiphany 1

Almighty God, who anointed Jesus at his baptism with
the Holy Spirit and revealed him as your beloved son;
inspire us, your children, who are born of water and
the Spirit, to surrender our lives to your service, that
we may rejoice to be called the sons and daughters of
God; through Jesus Christ our Lord.   Amen.

Strengthening: Epiphany 2

Almighty God, by whose grace alone we are accepted
and called to your service: strengthen us by your Holy
Spirit and make us worthy of our calling; through Jesus
Christ our Lord.   Amen.

Power: Epiphany 6

Heavenly Father, whose blessed son was revealed that
he might destroy the works of the devil and make us
the sons and daughters of God and heirs of eternal life:
grant that we, having this hope, may purify ourselves
even as he is pure; that when he shall appear in power
and great glory we may be made like him in his eternal
and glorious kingdom; where he is alive and reigns
with you and the Holy Spirit, one God, now and for
ever.   Amen.

Healing: 8 Before Easter

Almighty and everliving God, whose son Jesus Christ
healed the sick and restored them to wholeness of life:
look with compassion on the anguish of the world, and
by your healing power make whole both men and
nations; through our Lord and saviour Jesus Christ,
who is alive and reigns with you and the Holy Spirit,
one God, now and for ever.   Amen.

Reconditioning: 7 Before Easter

Merciful Lord, grant to your faithful people pardon and peace: that we may be cleansed from all our sins and serve you with a quiet mind; through Jesus Christ, our Lord.　Amen.

Love: Ash Wednesday

Almighty and everlasting God, you hate nothing that you have made and forgive the sins of all those who are penitent. Create and make in us new and contrite hearts, that, lamenting our sins and acknowledging our wretchedness, we may receive from you, the God of all mercy, perfect forgiveness and peace; through Jesus Christ our Lord.　Amen.

Steadfastness: Lent 2

Lord God Almighty, grant your people grace to withstand the temptations of the world, the flesh, and the devil, and with pure hearts and minds to follow you, the only God; through Jesus Christ our Lord.　Amen.

Example: Palm Sunday

Almighty and everlasting God, who in your tender love towards mankind sent your son our saviour Jesus Christ to take upon him our flesh and to suffer death upon the cross: grant that we may follow the example of his patience and humility, and also be made partakers of his resurrection; through Jesus Christ our Lord.　Amen.

Partners: Easter 2

God of peace, who brought again from the dead our Lord Jesus Christ, that great shepherd of the sheep, by the blood of the eternal covenant: make us perfect in every good work to do your will, and work in us that which is well pleasing in your sight; through Jesus Christ our Lord.　Amen

Trust: Easter 3

Almighty God, whose son Jesus Christ is the resurrection and the life of all who put their trust in him: raise us, we pray, from the death of sin to the life of righteousness; that we may seek the things which are above, where he reigns with you and the Holy Spirit, one God, now and for ever.   Amen.

Oneness: Easter 4

Almighty God, who alone can bring order to the unruly wills and passions of sinful men: give us grace, to love what you command and to desire what you promise, that in all the changes and chances of this world, our hearts may surely there be fixed where lasting joys are to be found; through Jesus Christ our Lord.   Amen.

Reassurance: Easter 5

Almighty and everlasting God, you are always more ready to hear than we to pray and give more than either we desire or deserve. Pour down upon us the abundance of your mercy, forgiving us those things of which our conscience is afraid and giving us those things which we are not worthy to ask save through the merits and mediation of Jesus Christ your son our Lord.   Amen.

Guidance: Whitsunday

Almighty God, who at this time taught the hearts of your faithful people by sending to them the light of your Holy Spirit: grant us by the same Spirit to have a right judgement in all things, and evermore to rejoice in his holy comfort; through the merits of Christ Jesus our saviour, who is alive and reigns with you in the unity of the Spirit, one God, now and for ever.   Amen.

Inspiration: Whitsunday

Almighty God, who on the day of Pentecost sent your
Holy Spirit to the disciples with the wind from heaven
and in tongues of flame, filling them with joy and
boldness to preach the Gospel: send us out in the
power of the same Spirit to witness to your truth and
to draw all men to the fire of your love; through Jesus
Christ our Lord.   Amen.

Direction: Trinity 5

Almighty God, without you we are not able to please
you. Mercifully grant that your Holy Spirit may in all
things direct and rule our hearts; through Jesus Christ
our Lord.   Amen.

Love: Trinity 6

Lord, you have taught us that all our doings without
love are nothing worth. Send your Holy Spirit and pour
into our hearts that most excellent gift of love, the true
bond of peace and of all virtues, without which
whoever lives is counted dead before you. Grant this
for the sake of your only son, Jesus Christ our
Lord.   Amen.

Opening: Trinity 7

Almighty God, who sent your Holy Spirit to be the life
and light of your Church: open our hearts to the riches
of his grace, that we may bring forth the fruit of the
Spirit in love and joy and peace; through Jesus Christ
our Lord.   Amen.

Protected: Trinity 8

Almighty God, you see that we have no power of
ourselves to help ourselves. Keep us both outwardly in
our bodies and inwardly in our souls, that we may be
defended from all adversities which may happen to the
body, and from all evil thoughts which may assault and
hurt the soul; through Jesus Christ our Lord.   Amen.

Guidance: Trinity 13

Lord God, the protector of all who trust in you, without whom nothing is strong, nothing is holy: increase and multiply upon us your mercy, that you being our ruler and guide, we may so pass through things temporal that we finally lose not the things eternal. Grant this, heavenly Father, for the sake of Jesus Christ our Lord. Amen.

Strengthening: Trinity 16

Lord of all power and might, the author and giver of all good things: graft in our hearts the love of your name, increase in us true religion, nourish in us all goodness, and of your great mercy keep us in the same; through Jesus Christ our Lord. Amen.

Perseverance: Trinity 18

Almighty and everlasting God, increase in us your gift of faith; that, forsaking what lies behind and reaching out to that which is before, we may run the way of your commandments and win the crown of everlasting joy; through Jesus Christ our Lord. Amen.

Inspiration: Trinity 21

Stir up, O Lord, the wills of your faithful people; that richly bearing the fruit of good works, they may by you be richly rewarded; through Jesus Christ our Lord. Amen.

Love: Last after Pentecost

Merciful God, you have prepared for those who love you such good things as pass man's understanding. Pour into our hearts such love towards you that we, loving you above all things, may obtain your promises, which exceed all that we can desire; through Jesus Christ our Lord. Amen.

Remaking: St Simon and St Jude

Almighty God, you have built your Church upon the foundation of the apostles and prophets with Jesus Christ himself as the chief cornerstone. So join us together in unity of spirit by their doctrine, that we may be made a holy temple acceptable to you; through Jesus Christ our Lord.   Amen.

Book of Common Prayer, adapted

COLOSTOMY

When faced with crisis or sudden need, I forget, Father, that you are there. Deep down I know that for Christ to be real I must invite him into my life, and let him be beside me in my deepest fears and sufferings.

Father, it seems so idiotic to be praying about my colostomy when I should be praying about my fear. I am afraid of the bag, afraid of its position, fearful of collision, fearful of others handling me. (And there is my fear of being more abnormal than ever.)

Father, if I keep giving in to fear there will not be much of me left — let alone the colostomy. Father you came to show a way through fear. You sent your son to pave light through darkness, in a new and most personal way. You sent your son to save and help, support and guide.

Now you send skilled doctors and nurses to give help and guidance. Let me trust now in you and respond to your messengers thankfully, through Jesus Christ our Lord.   Amen.

COMMANDMENTS

The ten commandments

1 Worship only God.
2 Do not make or take any images for yourself which you can worship.
3 Do not use God's name in a false or facetious or irreverent way.
4 Remember the sabbath day and keep it holy.
5 Honour your father and mother.
6 Do not kill.
7 Do not commit adultery.
8 Do not steal.
9 Do not give false evidence.
10 Do not desire what belongs to another.

Hear O Israel, the Lord our God, the Lord is one.

The Shema: Exodus 20; Deuteronomy 5

The two great commandments

1 Love the Lord your God with all your heart and all your soul, and all your might.

Deuteronomy 6:4f

2 Love your neighbour as yourself.

Leviticus 19:18

COMMITMENT

Commitment to Christ leads to life;
Commitment involves surrender;
Surrender is a willingness to give things up.

We draw lines, telling Christ how far
we will go.
Christ comes along and says
I want you to go further
And that makes the true cross in our own lives
— the going further.

Gordon Davies

COMMUNICATION

Starved of communication, starved of love.

COMPASSION

MacAskill sat very still, his head bent and his shoulders
a little slumped, and Judith noticed that his chest
hardly moved when he breathed. His mouth was a little
open and he looked frail and hurt. Involuntarily she
reached out her hand to his and touched him for a
moment as if to remind him he was not alone, and that
someone cared. She did it quite without embarrassment
for she felt a strength in herself she had not felt before
and she knew it was all right to touch him — much
more than that, it was *right* to.

He looked slowly round at her, his eyes no longer so
blank and staring as when she had first seen them, but
softer and younger, though bound by lines and
darkness of approaching old age. She smiled gently,
wondering why she wanted to do more, to hold him,
and yet not knowing how to start.

William Horwood, The Stonor Eagles

When Israel was a child I loved him,
   and out of Egypt I called my son.
The more I called them
   the more they went from me;
They kept sacrificing to Baals,
   and burning incense to idols.

Yet it was I who taught Ephraim to walk,
   I took them up in my arms;
But they did not know that I healed them.
I led them with cords of compassion
   with the bands of love,
And I became to them as one
   who eases the yoke on their jaws
And I bent down to them and fed them.

How can I give you up, O Ephraim!
   How can I hand you over, O Israel!
How can I make you like Admah!
   How can I treat you like Zeboi'im!
My heart recoils within me,
   my compassion grows warm and tender.

I will not execute my fierce anger,
   I will not again destroy Ephraim;
For I am God and not man,
   the Holy One in your midst,
And I will not come to destroy.

Hosea 11, Revised Standard Version (adapted)

COMPLACENCY, The danger of

I'm the fellow who goes into a restaurant, sits down and patiently waits while the waitresses finish their visiting before taking my order.

I'm the fellow who goes into a department store and stands quietly while the clerks finish their little chat.

I'm the fellow who drives into a service station and never blows his horn, but lets the attendant take his time.

You might say that I'm the good guy. But do you know who else I am?

I'm the fellow who never comes back.

It puzzles me to see business spending so much money every year to get my business — when I was there in the first place.

And all they needed to keep me coming back was to give me some service and extend a little courtesy.

Anonymous: 'The Good Guy'

COMPLAINING

There is so much good in the worst of us
And so much bad in the best of us
That it ill behoves any of us
To find fault with the rest of us.

Anonymous

Lord, as I find fault, others may hear in me the very things of which I complain in them.

I had no shoes, and complained, until I met a man who had no feet.

Arabian proverb

Are you going to let this day slip away useless?

CONFIDENCE

It is not the critical manner that elicits confidence from others, but the suggestion of trust and understanding.

Melville Harcourt 1909-1984, Thirteen for Christ

It is no use trusting in the Lord if you are careless.

Mollie Partridge

In others

Do not open your heart to the firm silent one; guard your tongue before the garrulous fool.

Chinese aphorism

CONFRONTATION

Grant me, Lord, the readiness to approach all
conflicting issues with a desire to understand; make me
helpful in criticism, slow to blame, quick to express
appreciation, and save me from unkind words and from
unkind silences.

So often, Lord, the demon I think I see in others is a
reflection of something needing deep resolution within
myself. Help me to know my adversary so that I may
truly understand and perceive.   Amen.

See also: Matthew 4:1-11; Luke 4:1-13

CONSIDER

When I consider how my light is spent . . .
                    John Milton 1609–1674, 'On His Blindness'

CONSIDERATION

Let us be patient, tender, wise, forgiving
   In this strange task of living
For if we fail each other, each will be
   Grey driftwood lapsing to the bitter sea.
                              Martin Armstrong

CONTENTMENT

Lord teach me to be content
by doing everything for you.

The best of blessings — a contented mind.
                              Horace 65–8BC

CONTROL

Lord what I find difficult, you found difficult too.
Thank you for the knowledge that I am not alone
and that you share the way with me, through
holding to your path and stepping into your
light.   Amen.

CONFIRMATION, Sacrament of

The sacrament of confirmation was originally performed by the bishop immediately after baptism (infant baptism began during the third century).

Through the laying on of hands, the bishop confers the gift of the Holy Spirit so that the confirmand may be fully empowered to carry out his or her vow to exercise complete responsibility within the Christian community. If followed sincerely this in turn will lead to full responsibility in relations at home and in all areas of life. Confirmation denotes a maturity of attitude and responsibility.

Vow

I turn to Christ
I repent of my sins
I renounce evil.

Alternative Service Book 1980

Creed

I believe in God the Father who has made me and all the world.
I believe in God the Son who has redeemed me and all mankind.
I believe in God the Holy Spirit who sanctifies me and all the people of God.

Southwark Diocese

Bishop's prayer

Almighty and everlasting God
you have given your servant(s) new birth
in baptism by water and the Spirit,
and have forgiven them all their sins.
Let your Holy Spirit rest upon them:
the spirit of wisdom and understanding;
the spirit of counsel and inward strength;
the spirit of knowledge and true godliness;
and let their delight be in the fear of
the Lord.   Amen.

Alternative Service Book 1980

Confirmation, sacrament of (ctd)

Individual's prayer

Defend me, O Lord, with your heavenly grace, that I
may continue yours for ever and daily increase in your
Holy Spirit more and more until I come to your
everlasting kingdom.   Amen.

Alternative Service Book 1980 (adapted)

Church's prayer

Eternal God
You have declared in Christ
the completion of your purpose of love.
May we live by faith, walk in hope,
and be renewed in love
until the world reflects your glory,
and you are all in all.
Even so; come, Lord Jesus.   Amen.

Alternative Service Book 1980, traditional

CO-OPERATION

Tubby Clayton, the founder of Toc H, said that
when he was visiting a friend in Kaano, he went
outside the city to visit the leper colony. After
travelling for some time he saw beside the road a
remarkable sight. In a field that was being sown,
he espied two men; one had no arms and the other
no legs. The man who had no arms was carrying
the man who had no legs; and the man who had
no legs was scattering the seed to sow the crop
which would feed the lepers.

COURAGE

To run from your demon is to have him pursue you.
Better to advance and meet him in his world than to
retreat and have him enter yours. Meet your demon.

Chinese aphorism

Do you have the courage to forgive?

Pilgrim:
When your ship
Long moored in harbour
Gives you the illusion
Of being a house;
When your ship begins to put down roots
In the stagnant water by the quay,
Put out to sea!
Save your boat's journeying soul
And your own pilgrim soul,
Cost what it may.

Archbishop Helder Camara

When the heart knows no danger, no danger exists.
When the soul becomes the warrior, all fear melts,
As the snowflake that falls upon your hand.

Chinese aphorism

Rejoice when thou dost see
God take thy things from thee;
When thy props are laid low
And friend turns to foe.
'Tis but because now
God seeth that thou
No longer on crutches must go.
Each here
Whom he setteth alone,
He himself is most near.

Bjornson, 'Strength'

Give me the courage, O God, in this quiet place
to face the things I ought to face.

Rita Snowden

Always seek, by preference, not the easiest, but the
    most difficult:
Not the most tasty, but the most insipid;
Not what pleases, but what afflicts;
Not what eases you, but what demands hard work;

Not more, but less;
Not the highest and most precious, but the lowliest and
    most despised;
Not the desire for anything, but the non-desire!
Not to seek the best in things, but the less good,
And to place oneself, for Jesus Christ's sake, in
    nakedness, emptiness
And poverty of all that the world contains.

First book of the Subida

O God, thou art our need. Strip fear from us as the
hunter strips skin from his game. Let us in nothing be
anxious. Let our courage be as steady as the giant
cottonwood, as penetrating as the harmattan wind, as
contagious as a child's laugh, for thou art our need.

Prayer from Africa

O God
you can make it tough
but please
don't make it
impossible.
Prayer of Uruguayan survivors of a plane crash in the Andes

Lord, may we have the courage to be straightforward in
this complicated world.

COVETING

It is so easy, to desire without thinking, to grab
without consideration.
    If I am to control my urge, then direct me Lord into
the ways you want and the tasks you desire.   Amen.

COWARDICE

One who in a perilous situation thinks with his legs.
Ambrose Bierce 1842–1914

To see what is right and not to do it is cowardice.
Confucius (K'ung Fu-tze) 551–479BC

DARKNESS

O dark, dark, dark amid the blaze of noon
Irrecoverably dark, total eclipse
Without all hope of day.

John Milton 1609–1674, 'Samson Agonistes'

When all within is dark
and former friends misprise;
From them I turn to you,
and find love in your eyes.

When all within is dark,
and I my soul despise;
From me I turn to you,
and find love in your eyes.

When all your face is dark;
and your just angers rise;
From you I turn to you,
and find love in your eyes.

Israel Abrahams 1858-1924, based on Ibn Gabirol

Be empowered in the Lord, in the might of his
strength. Put on the whole armour of God so that you
can withstand the craftiness of the devil. For ours is not
a fight against a physical enemy, but against the
powers and authorities, against the working intent of
darkness in the rulers of this world, against spiritual
wickedness in high places.

Therefore wear every piece of God's armour, so you
can stand your ground when evil is at its worst.

Ephesians 6:10f

The instruments of darkness tell us truths;
Win us with honest trifles, to betray 's
In deepest consequence.

William Shakespeare 1564–1616, Macbeth

Thou also shalt light my candle:
The Lord my God shall make my darkness to be light.

Psalm 18:28

Lighten our darkness we beseech thee, O Lord, and by
thy great mercy defend us from all perils and dangers
of this night; for the love of thy only Son, our saviour,
Jesus Christ.   Amen.

Evening Prayer, Book of Common Prayer

DAY

Lord
Help me to live this day
   quietly easily
To lean upon thy great strength
   trustfully restfully
To wait for the unfolding of thy will
   patiently serenely
To meet others
   peacefully joyously
To face tomorrow
   confidently courageously.

A prayer of St Francis 1181–1226

Fresh air
New morning
Fresh visions
New light
Fresh changes
New beginnings
Your wonderful
gifts to me.

Fresh breathing
New seeing
Fresh hearing
New tastes
Fresh touching
New knowing
Your natural
gifts to me.

Heavenly Father
Earthly guide

Heavenly Jesus
Earthly joy
Heavenly Spirit
Earthly way
Let me serve you
This new day.

DEATH

Fear of dying

Death is the separation of the soul from the body; that
is all. I am not afraid of a separation which will unite
me for ever with God.

St Thérèse of Lisieux 1873–1897

Spiritual combat:

1 Temptation against faith v. inspiration to faith
2 Temptation to despair v. inspiration against despair
3 Temptation to impatience v. inspiration to patience
4 Temptation to vainglory v. inspiration against
  vainglory
5 Temptation to get and keep v. Inspiration against
  getting and keeping.

W. Harry Rylands (adapted)

I fear not death but dying.

David Gray

It is true we cannot conquer death; we can, however,
conquer our fear of death.

Nikos Kazantzakis 1883–1957

The ties of human love are too exquisitely tender to be
harshly torn asunder without provoking acute pain.

Robert Falcon Scott 1868–1912

Those who wish to face the facts should be allowed to do so.

Robert Platt

Stop lying! You know and I know that I am dying. Then at least stop lying about it. But he never had the spirit to do it. This falsity around him and within him did more than anything else to poison his last days.

Leo Tolstoy 1828–1910

Hope must never die too far ahead of the patient.

Gerald J. Aronson

It is as natural to die as to be born.

Sir Francis Bacon 1561–1626

I don't mind dying because my bags are always packed.

Pope John XXIII, 1881–1963

Praying into my own death

Beforehand

Lord, help me beforehand to remember the following steps:

To place a card by my telephone or bed where key names, addresses and telephone numbers can be found. If I am on a prescription, to place details on a card with the name, address and telephone number of my doctor.

In preparing for death, if possible, to see that everything is left in good order, with details known to at least one member of my family and a solicitor. To make adequate provision of my property for my family and my friends. This includes housing for any dependants.

To make a will. This needs to be witnessed by 2 sane people over 18 who are not going to benefit from the will. If I don't make a will, legal and financial problems will arise for my survivors.

To realise that however well prepared I may be, my death will come as an emotional shock, and cause pain or even anger to the bereaved.

To realise that bereavement may imitate a pattern of pain or illness, and that each bereavement is different.

When dying

To ask, if possible, for the last rites, with anointing;
To say prayers together with my family or friends;
To place my trust in God, and commend my soul to
    him, through Jesus Christ our Lord.   Amen.

At death

Lord, I pray that at my death my next-of-kin, or closest friend or neighbour, will remember:

To call the doctor to certify my death. The doctor will say whether he can issue a certificate. If I die alone or in unusual circumstances, the coroner must be informed. The coroner will eventually issue the certificate: whoever takes charge of my body in such circumstances should ask the doctor for the coroner's 'phone number. Unless there are specific arrangements already made, the coroner's officer will arrange the removal of the body. If there is no special preference, the local priest or doctor or coroner can make helpful suggestions.

To call my local priest, minister or rabbi. He is familiar with procedure, able to give comfort, guidance and support, and help ease the burden.

To notify the police if my death is in suspicious or illegal circumstances.

To ask the priest, minister or rabbi to commend my soul to God, while waiting for the undertaker to arrive. This may or may not be beside my corpse.

To see, when the undertaker arrives, that one member of the family or someone authorised by them ensures that my corpse is removed, and that this be arranged as quietly as possible. I pray that the undertakers will arrive clean and tidy, talk quietly, and be fully sensitive to the needs of the family who, in turn, must realise that the undertaker has a job to do.

If a post-mortem is required, the undertaker, who is acting on behalf of the coroner, will remove my corpse to a hospital. I hope that the full details of the undertaker and the coroner will be asked for and given. Lord, I hope it is realised, that no death-certificate can be issued until the post-mortem has been completed, for no burial or cremation can take place without the certificate.

Registering the death

Lord, I pray that whoever * registers my death will remember that it must be done as soon as possible and *within 5 days* at the local office of the Register of Births, Marriages and Deaths, and that at the registering, certain details must be offered, my age and occupation, as well as the death certificate being offered in exchange for a copy being given, together with a disposal certificate so that funeral arrangements can be made, and a copy of the certificate of registration of the death so that insurance and other claims can be met. If the funeral is not going to take place within 14 days they must notify the registrar when registering the death.

*Next-of-kin, those knowing the circumstances of the death, parish priest or executor if he(she) is arranging the funeral, or person present at the death, or matron of home for elderly people.

Announcing the death

Lord, I pray that the undertakers will help with announcing my death, arranging the details of service in consultation with my local priest, minister or rabbi and the next-of-kin or closest friend or neighbour. I pray that the undertakers will also help with any other practical concerns.

Benefits or allowances

Lord, it is so easy in the midst of grief, to forget that benefits and allowances are available. Help those needing them to ask what these are.

The funeral

I am grateful that, if asked, the undertaker will handle all arrangements. These will include:

1 The date, time, and place of the funeral; but he will need to know —
2 Whether the service is to be in church, synagogue and/or at the crematorium or cemetery chapel,
3 Whether I wished for burial or cremation,
4 How many cars will be needed,
5 Whether there will be flowers and/or money given to some charitable cause or memorial.
6 I am glad the undertaker will notify my local priest, minister or rabbi who will arrange further details in consultation with my relatives.

Emotions

Father, I pray that those who mourn will ask for help;

That they will allow themselves to be helped by friends and relatives.

That they will be natural with their emotions by crying when they want, being alone if they wish, talking if they like, varying moods if they will.

That they will be prepared for feelings of almost any kind — aching, shock, pain, confusion, emptiness, regret ('if only . . .') and guilt, anger, relief, numbness, and many more symptoms.

That they will understand that it will take an average of up to two years to heal the wounds.

That no decision or action should be made in haste, and

That, if possible, unless it is imperative, no moving of house or from the area should take place within a year of my death.

The meaning of death

Death is one of two things: either the absence of all
being and sensation, or — and this is the common
belief — the translation of the soul into another place.

If it is the absence of all sensation like a sleep
untroubled by any dream, it will be a wonderful gain.
If that is the nature of death, I for one will count it a
gain. But if death is a journey to another place, what
could be more heartening than this?

And what would you not give to talk with old
friends? If this speculation is true, I am willing to die
many times.

Plato 428–347BC, The Apology of Socrates *(adapted)*

Our life and our work can never be quite tidily
finished. But this is only to say that the final 'Amen' to
our lives which alone can make them good, can only be
spoken by God; by God who spoke the 'Amen' to his
beloved son's life on earth, raised him from the dead,
and then by the Holy Spirit's power made his life and
his death endlessly fruitful for good, until the end of
time.

When we come to the end, therefore, let us commend
our spirits to God our creator and redeemer in faith,
believing that he who raised Jesus from the dead will
be able to take what we have done for him, whether
explicitly or implicitly, and will gather it into his
kingdom, to be in that kingdom that particular
enrichment of the kingdom's glory which our particular
life had to contribute.

For there is something which only you can bring into
the kingdom of God.

Therefore let us live this life to the greater glory of
God, say our 'Amen' when the end comes, and trust
that Almighty God from his side will forgive us, will
accept us in his beloved son, and will himself
pronounce upon our little life his own 'Amen'.

Eric Symes Abbott 1906–1983

Abide with me . . .
the darkness deepens, Lord with me abide.

Henry Francis Lyte 1793–1847

'Preparing for death' is not the other-worldly, pious
exercise stamped upon our minds by Victorian
sentimentality, turning away from the things of earth
for the things of 'heaven'. Rather, for the Christian it is
preparing for 'eternal life', which means real living,
more abundant life, which is begun, continued
through, not ended *now*. And this means it is about
quality of life not quantity. How long it goes on here is
purely secondary.

So preparing for eternity means really learning to
live, not just concentrating on keeping alive. It means
living it *up*, becoming *more* concerned with
contributing to and enjoying what matters most —
giving the most to life and getting the most from it,
while it is on offer.

Bishop John Robinson 1919–1983

Lord, she spent four years depressing everybody before
she died. She wore depression like an aura that clouded
and finally vanquished us all.

If only she had said, 'I am going to die: but up to
that moment I am really going to live', she might have
shone.

Please God, when it comes to my turn, provided I
know, give me the resilience of your blessed son and
help me to live fully till the end.   Amen.

Dying is an art, like everything else.

Sylvia Plath 1932–1963

Though I walk through the valley of the
   shadow of death,
I will fear no evil, for thou art with me.

Psalm 23:4

I have been so great a lover: filled my days so proudly
With the splendour of Love's praise.
The pain, the calm, and the astonishment,
Desire illimitable, and still content,
And all dear names men use to cheat despair,
For the perplexed and viewless streams that bear
Our hearts at random down the dark of life.
Now, ere the unthinking silence of that strife
Steals down, I would cheat drowsy death so far,
My night shall be remembered for a star
That outshone all the sons of all men's days.
Shall I not crown them with immortal praise
Whom I have loved.

Rupert Brooke 1887–1915

Do not go gentle into that good night
Rage, rage against the dying of the light.

Dylan Thomas 1914–1953,
'Do not go gentle into that good night'

Even if the doctor does not give you a year, even if he
hesitates about a month, make one brave push and see
what can be accomplished in a week.

Robert Louis Stevenson 1850–1894

As the tree's sap doth seek the root below
In winter, in my winter now I go
Where none but thee, the eternal root
Of true love I may know.

John Donne 1571–1631

Others delight in length of days;
I wait for the lover that I long for,
Death!

Prayer of Shirano, a Japanese leper

There are three conditions which often look alike
Yet differ completely, flourish in the same hedgerow:
Attachment to self and to things and to persons,
   detachment

From self and from things and from persons; and,
    growing between them, indifference
Which resembles the others as death resembles life,
Being between two lives — unflowering, between
The live and the dead nettle. This is the use of
    memory:
For liberation — not less of love but expanding
Of love beyond desire, and so liberation
From the future as well as the past.

What we call the beginning is often the end
And to make an end is to make a beginning.
The end is where we start from.

And any action
Is a step to the block, to the fire, down the sea's throat
Or to an illegible stone: and that is where we start.

With the drawing of this Love and the voice of this
    Calling
We shall not cease from exploration
And the end of all our exploring
Will be to arrive where we started
And know the place for the first time.

'And all shall be well and
All manner of thing shall be well'
When the tongues of flame are in-folded
Into the crowned knot of fire
And the fire and the rose are one.

                    T. S. Eliot 1888–1962, 'Little Gidding'

The life that I have is
all that I have,
And the life that I have
is yours.
The love that I have
of the life that I have
Is yours and yours
and yours.

A sleep I shall have

A rest I shall have,
Yet death will be
but a pause
For the peace of my years
in the long green grass
will be yours and yours
and yours.

Leo Marks

Democritus says there are countless worlds.
Marcus Tullius Cicero, 106–43BC

In my father's house are many wayside taverns-for-the-journey.

Jesus Christ

The life of God is over all, and over death itself.
Quaker Book of Discipline

Teach me your mood, O patient stars,
Who climb each night the ancient sky,
Leaving on space no shade, no scars,
No trace of age, no fear to die.

Ralph Waldo Emerson 1803–1882

O God, who hast in thy love kept me vigorously and
joyfully at work in days gone by, and dost now send
me joyful and contented into silence and inactivity;
grant me to find happiness in thee in all my solitary
and quiet hours. In thy strength, O God, I bid farewell
to all. The past thou knowest; I leave it at thy feet.
Grant me grace to respond to thy divine call; to leave
all that is dear on earth, and go out alone to thee.

Prayer of a priest in old age

Lord now lettest thou thy servant depart in peace.
Luke 2:29

I am the life and the love
that is perfected in death;
death of all earthly that is me
life of all spiritual that is you.

I am the life and the love
perfected in the dying
that forces a way through
self-seeking to the resurrection
of self-giving,
to be totally
other than self.
For I am the life and the love
says the Lord.

How do we not know that love of life is not an illusion
and that the dislike of death is not a young person's
losing his way and not knowing that he is really going
home?   *Chuang Tzu 369BC*

. . . calm of mind all passion spent.
                    John Milton 1608–1674, 'Samson Agonistes'

Who knows if life is death and death life.
                                    Euripides 480–406BC

I warmed my hands before the fire of life;
It sinks and I am ready to depart.
                        Walter Savage Landor 1775–1864

Even such is time, that takes in trust
Our youth, our joys, our all we have,
And pays us but with earth and dust;
Who in the dark and silent grave,
When we have wandered all our ways,
Shuts up the story of our days;
But from this earth, this grave, this dust
My God shall raise me up, I trust.
                        Sir Walter Raleigh 1552–1618,
                        written on the eve of his execution

A short dark passage to eternal light.
Sir William Davenant 1606–1668

They that love beyond the world cannot be separated
by it. Death cannot kill what never dies.
William Penn 1644–1718

Death is not the extinguishing of the light but the
putting out of the lamp because the dawn has come.
Rabindranath Tagore 1861–1941

... The wiser mind
Mourns less for what age takes away
Than what it leaves behind.
William Wordsworth 1770–1850

It is true that Dorian Gray never grew old. His tragedy
was that he never grew. Earthly immortality is a
pathetic mirage. Time will not stop. In an attempt to
stop it, one merely stunts oneself.   *Anonymous*

The secular cathedrals stand
Upon their valuable land
Frozen forever in a lie
Determined always to deny
That man is weak and has to die.
W. H. Auden 1907–1973

Read:

    Psalm   23 — for reassurance
    Psalm   27 — for affirmation
    Psalm   51 — for contrition
    Psalm 121 — for enlightenment
    Psalm 139 — for pervasiveness

Eye has not seen, nor ear heard, nor the heart of man
conceived, what God has prepared for those who love
him.

1 Corinthians 2:9

If it's heaven for climate, it's hell for company.
Sir James Barrie 1860–1937

Only the fact of death puts the question of life's
meaning in all its depth.   *Nicolai Berdyaev 1874–1948*

The death of another

(Sentences for saying at home, in the hospital, for individual
and family prayers, in church or at the funeral parlour)

Rest eternal grant unto him (her) O Lord, and let light
perpetual shine upon him (her).

Book of Common Prayer

I am the resurrection and the life, says the Lord. He
that believes in me, though he were dead, yet shall he
live, and whosoever lives and believes in me shall
never die.   *John 11:25-26*

I know that my redeemer lives, and that he shall stand
at the last day upon the earth. Whom I shall see for
myself, and my eyes shall behold, and not another.
Job 19:25-27

We brought nothing into this world, and it is certain
we can carry nothing out. The Lord gave, and the Lord
has taken away; blessed be the name of the Lord.
1 Timothy 6:7; Job 1:21

The eternal God is thy refuge and underneath are the
everlasting arms.   *Deuteronomy 33:27*

Blessed are they that mourn; for they shall be
comforted.   *Matthew 5:4*

Let not your heart be troubled; you believe in God,
believe also in me.   *John 14:1*

I am persuaded that nothing in all creation shall be able
to separate us from the love of God, which is in Christ
Jesus our Lord.   *Romans 8:37f*

God so loved the world that he gave his only beloved son to the end that whosoever believes in him shall never perish, but have eternal life.   *John 3:16*

Love is not changed by death and nothing is lost and all in the end is harvest.   *Edith Sitwell 1887–1964*

Eternal God, you have taught us that our bodies are living temples of your spirit. As you have given, so you receive again those who are yours, hallowed in friendship, blessed in peace, and made eternal in your infinite love.

You, O Lord, are the endless power that renews life beyond death; you are the greatness that saves.
Daily Amidah (Standing Prayer)
Forms of Prayer for Jewish Worship

Blessed are you Lord, who renews life beyond death.
Daily Amidah (Standing Prayer)
Forms of Prayer for Jewish Worship

Of a colleague

Lord, I worked with N and shared so much in the tasks that were set before us. And now that he (she) is dead I mourn the loss and the regret of further insights shared and tasks unfulfilled. Yet I remember that through the example of your blessed son, quality of time and occasion means so much more than years; and what is unfulfilled can be given to others to complete.

Help me therefore, in my grief, to treasure what was given and not yearn for what was incomplete. For all will be completed in you, even my aching and my regrets; through Jesus Christ our Lord.   Amen.

Of a friend

A friend is the best of gifts, blessed through giving, blessed through sharing, blessed by acceptance through you. In the deep chasm of my grief help me to fill the aching with two further gifts, dear Lord: thankfulness

for the blessings of joys shared and truths revealed, and
the strength to live in the way that brought delight to
our friendship; through Jesus Christ our Lord.   Amen.

Of a husband

He was to me my other soul, who drew me closer every
day by an undemanding love. His joy was like the
morning sun, his passion like the blaze of noon, his
gentleness like the touch of evening; and now all his
creative powers are gathered into your darkness which
in turn will become your gift of another day. Thank
you Lord for our days and years, blessed by your
love.   Amen.

Of a wife

As the small pebbles beautify a stream,
as the leaves adorn a spreading tree,
as rays of light illuminate the morning sky,
so was my love.
How will the joys be shared, the laughing gathered;
the nearness of warmth,
the vacant space,
the yearning to give,
day by day and night by night,
be filled by her going?
No, Lord, I know they will not.
Only your great and supervening love
which always was and always will be,
can help me now,
and in time enable me to accept
what was so beautiful and true.
And I love her still,
in your safekeeping evermore.   Amen.

A cot death

Lord, I keep asking about my child, What did I do wrong? What have I done? Why? Why me?

In other moments I ask you to give me strength and courage and endurance to bear my heavy cross with the strength and courage and endurance of your only son, and to work through these into the quieter more accepting ways where you can lead me. Amen.

Of a child (for parents)

O God, we thank you for the loan of this child, *N*

For the joy of his (her) presence in our home,
For the privilege of loving and caring for him (her).
Today, our sorrow is your joy
And his (her) spirit returns into your care.

Grant us strength
To relinquish him (her) without grief,
In the sure knowledge,
That we shall be reunited with him (her),
In that other world, where all your children
Enjoy complete health of mind and spirit. Amen.

Anonymous

Of a young person

My life will be sour grapes and ashes without you.
Daisy Ashford 1881–1972, The Young Visitors

So full of life, so bright with promise, and now no more. Lord fill the void of our grief with deep thankfulness for *N* whom we love but see no longer, and fulfil your earthly promises with him (her) in heaven above, through your only son, Jesus Christ our Lord. Amen.

Where there is no body

Father we loved *N*, but cannot see his (her) body. In the tragedy of this situation let us who mourn remember *N* as he (she) was, and at his (her) best. The empty tomb has become a bed of hope for all who believe and trust in your risen son.

Help us now who cannot see the dead body to trust in your infinite power to redeem, through Jesus Christ the risen Lord.   Amen.

Of an outcast

Yet all is well; he has but passed
To life's appointed bourne:
And alien tears will fill for him
Pity's long broken urn,
For his mourners will be outcast men
And outcasts always mourn.

Oscar Wilde 1854–1900

By accident

Lord, so many elements are needed for enabling us to be born and grow to maturity. Every day in that process is filled with risk, every moment a possibility of benefit or loss.

Help us in this time of sudden loss and deep shock to trust in your sustaining strength and redeeming power. Comfort us and, by your cross and passion, show us the way, through darkness to light.   Amen.

By murder

Forgive, Lord, the perpetrator(s) of this savage act, and comfort us who mourn. It is so difficult to understand such needless waste, so hard to feel the forgiveness that must be realised if healing is to come, so terrifying to think of the cost, yet your Son took to himself the fullness of pain and deep-stinging death, and in his supreme sacrifice expunged the power of sin and transcended evil.   Amen.

By violence

Lord, I feel such rage at this cruelty, this needless spoiling, this desecration of your gift. Even more than my helpless pain, I feel for those who remain to live

with the consequences; for this sin has pained deep
roots in us all. This deed holds up a mirror of the
perpetrator's mind and soul.

Only your infinite forgiveness, in and through us,
can begin to heal the wounds. Begin, Lord,
now. Amen.

After a brief marriage

Well, Lord, she's dead. Clyde's wife.
And only twenty-five with but three married years and
    babies.
Can you see his loneliness, Lord?
He wanders about the house and it's empty.
No, that's not the word.
It's barren.
Where once had flowered loveliness, there's now a scar.
And the tearing of the roots makes his heart bleeding
    and raw.
The vacuum of his future seems to stretch for him in a
    chain of empty tomorrows.
Can you tell him, Lord, it won't always be like this?
Can you tell him, Lord, that he's had his gift?

The gift of pure love in a short life together.
Blooming quickly from bud to flower, and then,
not taken,
but made perfect and stored in all its young loveliness
deep within his very being
where nothing can change or mar.
Can you tell him, Lord, that out of all this pain,
you are there, among all of us who watch and wait.
Close by.
To hold and sustain.
And above all to resurrect the indomitable spirit of
    man.
Through your son, Jesus Christ. Amen.

Roger Bush

Of a non-Christian

We give profound thanks for N and his (her) life. As light and darkness are part of each day and both together nourish life, so we give thanks for the fullness of his (her) life, that what was excellent will be treasured and what was lacking will be perfected in our love and thankfulness.

Of Jews

Let us magnify and let us sanctify the great name of God in the world which he created according to his will. May his kingdom come in your lifetime and in your days, and the lifetime of all the family of Israel; quickly and speedily may it come.   Amen.

May the greatness of his being be blessed from eternity to eternity. Let us bless and let us extol,
> Let us tell aloud and let us raise aloft,
> Let us set on high and let us honour,
> Let us exalt and let us praise the Holy One.

Blessed be he, though he is far beyond any blessing or song, any honour or any consolation that can be spoken of in this world . . .   Amen.

May great peace from heaven and the gift of life be granted to us and to all the family of Israel.   Amen.

May he who makes peace in the highest bring peace to us and to all Israel.   Amen.

> *The Kaddish (the Sanctification),*
> *traditional Jewish prayer at death*

Psalms 23, 90, 130

We remember our six million dead, who died when madness ruled the world and evil dwelt on earth. We remember those we knew, and those whose very name is lost.

We mourn for all that died with them; their goodness and their wisdom, which could have saved the world

and healed so many wounds. We mourn for the genius
and the wit that died, the learning and the laughter
that were lost. The world has become a poorer place
and our hearts become cold as we think of the
splendour that might have been.

We stand in gratitude for their example of decency
and goodness. They are like candles which shine from
the darkness of those years, and in their light we know
what goodness is — and evil.

We salute those men and women who were not Jews,
who had the courage to stand outside the mob and
suffer with us. They, too, are your witnesses, a source
of hope when we despair.

Because of our people's suffering, may such times
never come again, and may their sacrifice not be in
vain. In our daily fight against cruelty and prejudice,
against tyranny and persecution, their memory gives us
strength and leads us on.

In *silence* we remember those who sanctified his
name on earth.

Forms of Prayer for Jewish Worship

Of non-believers

O dark dark dark. They all go into the dark,
The vacant interstellar spaces, the vacant into the
    vacant,
The captains, merchant bankers, eminent men of letters.
The generous patrons of art, the statesmen and the
    rulers,
Distinguished civil servants, chairmen of many
    committees,
Industrial lords and petty contractors, all go into the
    dark,
. . .
I said to my soul, be still, and let the dark come upon
    you
Which shall be the darkness of God. As, in the theatre,
The lights are extinguished, for the scene to be changed
With a hollow rumble of wings, with a movement of

darkness on darkness,
And we know that the hills and the trees, the distant
  panorama
And the bold imposing facades are all being rolled
  away —
Or as, when an underground train, in the tube, stops
  too long between stations
And the conversation rises and slowly fades into
  silence
And you see behind every face the mental emptiness
  deepen
Leaving only the growing terror of nothing to think
  about;
Or when, under ether, the mind is conscious but
  conscious of nothing —
I said to my soul, be still, and wait without hope
For hope would be hope for the wrong thing; wait
  without love
For love would be love of the wrong thing; there is yet
  faith
But the faith and the love and the hope are all in the
  waiting
Wait without thought, for you are not ready for
  thought:
So the darkness shall be the light, and the stillness the
  dancing.

T. S. Eliot 1888–1965, 'East Coker III'

Of Christians

Father of all, we pray to you for N whom we love, but
see no longer. Grant him (her) thy peace; let light
perpetual shine upon him (her); and in thy loving
wisdom and almighty power work in him (her) the
good purpose of thy perfect will; through Jesus Christ
our Lord.   Amen.

Book of Common Prayer

Heavenly Father, who in thy son Jesus Christ, has
given us a true faith and a sure hope: help us to live as
those who believe and trust in the communion of
saints, the forgiveness of sins, and the resurrection to
life everlasting; and strengthen this faith and hope in
us all the days of our life, through the love of thy son,
Jesus Christ our saviour.   Amen.

Book of Common Prayer

Bring us Lord at our last awakening to where there
shall be no darkness nor dazzling, but one equal light;
no noise nor silence, but one equal music; no fears nor
hopes, but one equal possession; no ends nor
beginnings, but one equal eternity, world without
end.   Amen.

Traditional

Some people will ask: 'How is the resurrection
achieved? And with what sort of body?'

In your own experience you know that a seed does
not germinate without itself 'dying'. When you sow a
seed, you do not sow the 'body' that will eventually be
produced, but bare grain — of wheat, for example, or
some other seed. God gives the seed a 'body' according
to *his* laws, and a different 'body' to each kind of seed.

Even in this world, all flesh is not the same. There is
a distinct difference between the flesh of human
beings, animals, fish and birds. There are bodies which
exist in this world, and which exist in the heavens.
These bodies are not, as it were, in competition; the
splendour of an earthly body is quite different from the
splendour of a heavenly body. The sun, the moon and
the stars all have their own particular splendour, while
among the stars themselves there are different kinds of
splendour.

So it is with the resurrection of the dead. What is
sown in the earth as a perishable thing is raised
imperishable. Sown in humiliation, it is raised in glory;

sown in weakness, it is raised in power; sown as an animal body, it is raised as a spiritual body.

When our mortality has been clothed with immortality, then the saying of scripture will come true: 'Death is swallowed up; victory is won'. 'O Death, where is your victory? O Death, where is your sting?'

But thanks be to God who gives us the victory over all these things through Jesus Christ our Lord.

I Corinthians 15 (adapted)

Death and life in perspective

Father, I am grateful that you are not a puppeteer. You do not manipulate people's deaths. You give each of us life, and then allow us the freedom to live it. Sadly that precious gift is often abused by nations, communities, individuals, and especially ourselves. Forgive us, Lord, with your deepest forgiveness. Amen.

A father loves his children whether they are good or bad. If a child truly loves he will wish to thank the father and honour their friendship. He will wish to benefit from being nearer the father.

If a child rebels and mars or hurts the father's gift, the father will not be less loving: the rebel will punish himself by not enjoying the father's love, which he could have if he followed the father's wise and most loving advice.

So are we with you, heavenly Father. Amen.

Father, you give us life, and allow us time in which to live. You neither promise more nor less life to the good or the bad. In fact, we are all mixtures of good and bad, of weakness and possibility. Heavenly Father, what is good please strengthen, and what is bad please redeem, and guide us all into the beauty of your peace, through Jesus Christ our Lord. Amen.

Heavenly Father, the atheists, who are your children,

say you do not exist, while those who are agnostic say they do not know. But I wish to give you profound thanks that death for a Christian is unnatural. I know that the body and the soul which have been a unity, separate. The pleasures of the body have given delight and for these I am most grateful; while the pains of the body have deepened my compassion and understanding, and my awareness that it is not all that is seen that has value.

Help me to perceive in death that as the shell of the body dies, the spirit which expressed life through the body, returns to you. Father keep me in the knowledge that the resurrection is not a return to the old body in revived form, but a passing up into new life with you, as different as the caterpillar is to the cocoon and the chrysalis to the butterfly.

In your infinite power to redeem with love and reunite with mercy, bring us to your heavenly kingdom and unite us with all whom we have known and loved. In this way the promises of Christ may be fulfilled, even when we are weak, and when faith is perfected through death, in Jesus Christ our Lord. Amen.

Bereavement

Bereavement is like a bandaged wound. The air of truth must come to it sufficiently for healing to begin. Yet it must not be so continually open that it is reinfected with false blame and needless guilt. But, like a wound, the pain and the hurt and achingness must be endured for the wound to be healed, even if the scar remains.

And just as wounds itch before the final healing so too we must leave some things at deeper levels to be healed in God's own time. Amen.

Father of mercy and giver of all comfort, deal graciously, we pray, with those who mourn, that, casting off every care on you they may know the consolation of your love, through Jesus Christ our Lord. Amen.

Book of Common Prayer

Lead him (her) forwards in peace from this world into
the life that has no end, supported by his (her) own
good deeds, and accompanied by my love. Help me
too, and teach me that though we may part now, we
shall come together once again in the gathering of life.

Forms of Prayer for Jewish Worship

He that lacks time to mourn, lacks time to mend.

Sir Henry Taylor 1800–1886

Death and bereavement are part of the universal
experience, as old as time, as multitudinous as the
myriad grains of sand on all the beaches of all the
oceans of the world, and yet as unique to the
individual as that individual is also unique. Between
those who have died and the bereaved a web of
relationships exists; yet each strand is in itself unique,
and that unique relationship has to be dealt with
before the bereavement can be lived through
successfully and be made a part of the wholeness of the
survivor.

Barbara Bunce and Beryl Statham, About Bereavement

We seem to give them back to you, O God, who gave
them to us . . . Yet as you did not lose them in giving,
so we do not lose them by their return. O lover of
souls, you do not give as the world gives. What you
give you do not take away; for what is yours is ours
also if we are yours. And life is eternal and love is
immortal; and death is only a horizon; and a horizon is
nothing save the limit of our sight. Lift us up, strong
son of God, that we may see further; cleanse our eyes
that we may see more clearly; draw us closer to yourself
that we may know ourselves to be nearer to our loved
ones who are with you. And while you prepare a place
for them, prepare us also for that happy place, that
where you are we may be also for evermore.   Amen.

Bishop Charles Henry Brent 1862–1929 (adapted)

I stood watching as the little ship sailed out to sea. The
setting sun tinted her white sails with a golden
light . . . and as she disappeared from sight a voice at
my side whispered, 'He is gone'.

But the sea was a narrow one. On the farther shore a
little band of friends had gathered to watch and wait in
happy expectation. Suddenly they caught sight of the
tiny sail and, at the very moment when my companion
had whispered, 'He is gone', a glad shout went up in
joyous welcome, 'Here he comes'.

Anonymous

Lord Haldane said that it is in *devotion* to this search
after the Most High — a search which may assume an
infinity of varied forms — that the dedicated life
consists: that life is not to be judged by apparent
failure to reach some fixed and rigid goal, but rather by
the *quality* of *striving*.

And, when he shall die,
Take him and cut him out in little stars,
And he will make the face of heaven so fine
That all the world will be in love with night
And pay no worship to the garish sun.

William Shakespeare 1563–1616, Romeo and Juliet

DECEIT

O what a tangled web we weave
When first we practice to deceive.

Sir Walter Scott 1771–1832

O man, strange composite of heaven and hell,
Who never art so near to shame
As when thou hast achieved some deed of fame.

John Henry Newman 1801–1890

DEDICATION

In thy service may we live, and in thy service may we die, through Jesus Christ our Lord.   Amen.

Bishop Brooke Foss Westcott 1825–1901

DEFEAT

Lord, help me to see defeat as a change of course, and not an end in itself.

The only real death is the death we die every day by not living.

Nikos Kazantzakis 1883–1957, Zorba the Greek

To die well one must live well: your life cries out to be lived.   *Chinese aphorism*

DELAYING, Danger in

He was going to be all that he wanted to be —
tomorrow.
No one would be kinder or nicer than he — tomorrow.
A friend who was tired and weary he knew would be
glad of a lift, and who needed it too, on him he
would call and see what he would do — tomorrow.

Each morning he would stack up the letters he'd write
— tomorrow.
And think of the friends he would fill with delight —
tomorrow.
It was a pity he was busy today and hadn't a moment
to stop on his way, more time I'd give to others,
he'd say — tomorrow.

This greatest of wonders the world would have known
— tomorrow.
His friends would have seen him had he ever known
— tomorrow.
But he vanished from sight and he faded from view
and all that he left here when living was through
a mountain of things he intended to do — tomorrow.

Anonymous

Delay is the deadliest form of denial.

From Parkinson's law

Procrastination is the thief of time.   *Anonymous*

Deviate an inch, lose a thousand miles.

Anonymous

DELIGHT

Delight in the Lord
And he shall give thee thy heart's desire.

Psalm 37:4

DELIVERANCE

Within yourself deliverance must be sought.

William Blake 1757–1827

None of us belongs to darkness or the night. Let us
then never fall into the sleep that stupefies the rest of
the world: let us keep awake, with our wits about us.
Night is the time for sleep and the time when men get
drunk, but we men of the daylight should be alert, with
faith and love as our breastplate and the hope of our
salvation as our helmet. For God did not choose us to
condemn us, but that we might secure salvation
through Jesus Christ our Lord.

1 Thessalonians 5:4-9 JBP

It is high time to awake out of sleep: for now is our
salvation nearer than when we first believed. The night
is far spent, the day is at hand: let us therefore cast off
the works of darkness and let us put on the armour of
light. Let us walk honestly, as in the day.

Romans 13:11-13, Authorised Version

Awake thou that sleepest, and Christ shall give thee
light.   *Ephesians 5:14, Authorised Version*

It is the Spirit that gives life, the flesh is of no avail.
John 6:63, Revised Standard Version

The kingdom of God is within you.
Luke 17:21, Authorised Version

DENTIST, A visit to the

Lord of all power and might be with me at this time.
Quietly and calmly let me trust in the skill and
gentleness of this dentist who in caring for my teeth
helps me to understand more fully the need to care
consistently and well for all your gifts, to me and to
others.

Help me to accept discomfort and discipline, so that a
restored mouth and a clean mouth may give thanks and
praise to your holy name.   Amen.

DEPRESSION

In the midst of winter I finally learned that there was in
me an invincible summer.
Albert Camus 1913–1960

Sometimes I battle with depression. I never know all
the reasons for this 'dark pit', as it seems to me. Some
of it may be hurt pride. Sometimes it is obviously
exhaustion, physical, mental, emotional and spiritual.
At times, when I am tired and strained, I can get angry
over an incident that may be quite trivial in itself; and
then I get angry with myself for getting angry. As I
suppress both forms of anger, depression is the result. I
am then even more difficult to live with than usual. I
do not want people to get too near to me, but I hope
very much that they will not go too far away either.
David Watson 1933–1984, You are My God

Calvary would seem to be the moral crisis of the world
focused down to one terrific apocalypse.
Richard Roberts

DESPAIR

Most men live lives of quiet desperation.

Henry David Thoreau 1817–1862

Lord, it is dark.
Lord, are you here in my darkness?

Your light has gone out, and so has its
reflection on men and on all things and me.

It wouldn't matter, except I am alone.
I am alone.
You have taken me far, Lord; trusting,
I followed you, and you walked at my side.
And now, at night, in the middle of the
desert, suddenly you have disappeared.
I call and you do not answer.
I search and I do not find you.
I have left everything, and now am left alone.
Your absence is my suffering.

Lord, it is dark.
Lord, are you here in my darkness?

Michel Quoist

DESPERATION

The lowest ebb is the turning of the tide.

Henry Wadsworth Longfellow 1807–1882

When cold and hunger come upon men, honesty and
shame depart. *Ch'ao Ts'o*

DEVOTION

True devotion is never a melancholy deed either for
itself or for others.

Sir Thomas Browne 1605–1682

DIAGNOSIS

Prepared for either event. *Virgil 70–19BC*

DIFFICULTY

Father, your way is an infinite line proceeding from
divine love and ending in divine fulfilment. You have
shown the way in following your son, Christ Jesus.

Help me to follow him truly each day. And although
I shall stray, because it is in my nature to vary and be
inconsistent, draw me back with gentleness and love,
so that nothing may seem too difficult in response to
your call, through Jesus Christ our Lord.   Amen.

In speaking

When the time comes the words you need will be given
you, for it is not you who will be speaking, it will be
the spirit of your father speaking in you.

Matthew 10:19-20

In communication

I can't hear what you say because I am deafened by
what you are.

Anonymous

DIGESTION

Thank you Lord for the means of digesting food, the
means of giving strength to my body, the power to
distribute efficiently and well from what has been
given.

Help me, Lord, to be thankful and to learn from the
inside, lessons for the outside, and, most of all, to value
your precious gift. Teach me to eat neither fast nor
slowly, but trust calmly and caringly in your strength to
guide and sustain, through Jesus Christ our
Lord.   Amen.

DISAPPEARED, The

A child

Father, from the first hours of his (her) disappearance,

my heart was taken from me and I sank into desperate expectancy and despair. No familiar sight or sound of him (her). No sparkle. No mischief. No sudden tenderness. No unsolicited love.

Help me Father, to accept this bitter bitter blow. If *N* is no more, bring me to accept this fact; and if he (she) is alive, then please speed his (her) safe return; through Jesus Christ your only son our Lord.   Amen.

Political victims

Father, I am praying for the poor bruised victims of humanity who live lives of quiet desperation, in poverty, disease, violence and neglect; they protest and then quietly disappear, for ever.

Any of those people could be me. I feel deeply inadequate. Help me, Father, to support those people who truly seek to bring the light of your truth to all those in the darkness of oppression and the shadow of death; through Jesus Christ our Lord.   Amen.

Lord, forgive the social sin of the First World.

DISAPPOINTMENT

Lord I am so disappointed.
Hours and hours were spent
in producing the right colour
the right atmosphere to
make this painting the perfect gift.
And so it was but for
one essential thing.
He is colour-blind.

Next time, Lord, give me the
courage and wisdom
to think more before
doing much,
however good the performance,
however excellent the result.

I realise now that form
is pleasing but
substance is all.

DISCIPLINE

Discipline your body that you may find greater power.
Discipline your mind that you may have greater joy.

Chinese aphorism

DISEASE

Meet the disease as it approaches.

A. P. F. Persius 34–62 AD

O Lord God, our heavenly Father, whose hand is ever
stretched out in blessing and healing upon the sick, we
pray for the work of the Cystic Fibrosis Research Trust.

Grant that through the skill and patience of doctors
and nurses, children and young people who suffer may
be set free from the sickness which affects them; grant
to all parents compassion and understanding and that
by thy blessing upon them and upon all who try and
help them, they may find encouragement and peace.

Through Jesus Christ our Lord.   Amen.

Cystic Fibrosis Research Trust

DISFIGUREMENT

'Tis true my form is something odd,
But blaming me is blaming God;
Could I create myself anew
I would not fail in pleasing you.

If I could reach from pole to pole
Or grasp the ocean with a span,
I would be measured by the soul;
The mind's the standard of the man.

Isaac Watts 1674–1748

Lord, they dread my skin as I dread their eyes.

Lord, in giving me so much disfigurement give me the
strength to carry this cross and endure, in the example
of your only son. In spite of my disguise help the
essential me to be seen, and give me so much greater
compassion for all who suffer; through Jesus Christ our
Lord.   Amen.

Once, when referring to his own appearance, he said:
'It *is* very strange for, you see, mother was so beautiful.'
Michael Howell and Peter Ford, The True History of the
Elephant Man

DOCTORS

In this time of need, I ask you most sincerely Lord, to
guide this doctor in fulfilling the skills he (she) has
learnt, the patience he (she) has acquired and the care
and kindness that can put me at my ease. Let his (her)
peace be your peace, his (her) words your words and
his (her) hands your hands, for Christ's sake.   Amen.

God and the doctor we alike adore
But only when in danger, not before;
The danger o'er, both are alike requited,
God is forgotten, and the doctor slighted.
John Owen 1560–1622, Epigrams

DONATION (of body to science)

Lord in the right hands you have given science to be
an instrument of knowledge and benefit to mankind.
We pray that those who give their bodies for scientific
investigation that is of benefit to others may in you
repose safe in the knowledge that their souls are not
hindered from the nearness of your presence and the
joy of everlasting life.

Grant to all who pioneer new benefits in medicine,

and those who receive them, sensitive and lasting
appreciation of the same, and may those who have
given be gifted with the joys and certainty of selfless
love now and through eternity for Jesus' sake.   Amen.

Parents of donors

If eyes can see anew,
if kidneys and liver can save lives,
if healthy organs can live on in others,
then take my dead child's body
and make out of *my* nothing
something more, dear Lord,
something good by which he (she) can be remembered,
and an aspect of resurrection through giving,
in the example of your only Son, who is life beyond
   death.   Amen.

DREAMS

All men have dreams of different types, good and bad.
There are the vain dreams, futile, based on faceless
hopes. There are the dreams that spur and inspire,
based on aspiration to a high ideal. And there are the
false dreams based on lies, to oneself, or others.

Chinese

DRIVING

Teach those who drive, O Lord, the spirit of humility
and patience. May they realise that there is nothing to
be gained from fast and careless driving except death
and injury and heartache. Help us all to see that bad
driving habits can turn a means of transport into a
weapon of death and destruction as diabolical as the
gun and the bomb. Hear us, O Lord, when we call
upon you for a safe journey. And help us truly to give
thanks when we arrive at our destination in safety.

Teach us all respect for the law, for the rule of the
road, and for the rights of other road users.

Help us to put our Christian faith into practice in the way that we drive so that we may set a good example.

Prayer following the death of the elder son of a Nigerian clergyman in a motor accident

Drive prayerfully
Look carefully
And thoughtfully
Every time.

DRUGS

Lord, you have given to men and women the skill to make drugs, and to use them wisely. In their effectiveness to relieve and strengthen (*or* to ease pain and discomfort, bruises and swellings), let those who administer and those who use your drugs, honour them as your gift until quietened and relieved of suffering they rejoice in your power which saves and your love which redeems. Amen.

To many, total abstinence is easier than perfect moderation.

Sir Francis Bacon 1561–1626

Lord teach me to be dependent on you and not on drugs, to find myself in you and not false alternatives, and to see the gift of life, honoured and cherished, as the way to true reality and abiding joy. Amen.

Lord, I am dependent on drugs. They ease my suffering and calm my fears. Help me to use wisely what I receive and value the care that is needed in administering them well, through him who heals and saves, even Jesus Christ our Lord. Amen.

EASTER

Easter light:
Easter joy.
You bring the promise of sunlight,
   the resurgence of hope;
For in you *all* has been conquered,
   death and pain and doubt;
All has been fulfilled in you,
   love and faith and life.
For you are
Easter light:
Easter joy.

EDUCATION

Education begins a man, but reading, good company,
and reflection must finish him.

John Locke 1632–1704

O father give me passport
O mother give me passport
Elder brother give me passport
To job and life
Give me education.

Prayer of a Ugandan Christian

If you give a man a fish, he will eat once.
If you teach a man to fish, he will eat for the rest of his
   life.
If you are thinking a year ahead, sow seed.
If you are thinking ten years ahead, plant a tree.
If you are thinking one hundred years ahead, educate
   the people.
By sowing the seed you will harvest once.
By planting a tree, you will harvest tenfold.
By educating the people you will harvest one
   hundredfold.

Kuang-tsu, 4th–3rd century BC

Lord, education is a life-long experience leading us forth from where we are to where you would have us be, in the example of your living word Jesus. Help us to deepen our knowledge and understanding, our awareness and sensitivity, our discipleship to you and our serving others in your name, through Jesus Christ our Lord. Amen.

EFFORT

Before the gates of excellence lies always the high road of sweat.   *Anonymous*

Never give in! Never, never, never, never — in nothing great or small, large or petty — never give in except to convictions of honour and good sense.
                                    Winston Churchill 1874–1965

Nothing of any value is ever achieved without sustained application.

Heroic toil and silence and endurance lead to the high places of the universe.
                                    Thomas Carlyle 1795–1881

EGOISM

The enthroned egoist is often a very grim person who assaults life with energetic, yet purposeless activity and busyness. Inwardly he is desperate. And serious. He feels that his life demands his constant attention. To relax, to let things happen, to stop worrying and take a nap — these suggestions are abhorrent to his life. He is eternally busy, working and worrying his way through life. He feels it all depends on him.
                                    Earl Jabay, The God Players

ELDERLY, The

There is nothing more charming than a warm spirit in an elderly body.

God hideth his intention.
God knows. His will
Is best. The stretch of years
Which wind ahead, so dim
To our imperfect vision,
Are clear to God. Our fears
Are premature: In him
All time hath full provision.

Minnie Louise Haskins 1875–1937

Lord I am old in body but young in spirit. Help me to
accept with dignity and grace the limits of my body.
Science assures me that from my twenties I begin to
decline; yet freed from passion to be deepened in love,
I now find greater and deeper value in what I can
appreciate and do. For, you assure me everlastingly that
my soul can expand into ever broader horizons as my
trust grows in you; through Jesus Christ our
Lord.   Amen.

Lord I am glad that though I was young and smooth
and now am old and wrinkled, my essential nature has
not changed. And my need of you is real.
    As you empty this earthen vessel fill me with your
transcendent life, your flowing spirit and your eternal
love, for Jesus Christ's sake.   Amen.

A good man feels old age more by the strength of his
soul than the weakness of his body.

Sir Thomas Overbury 1581–1613

ENDURANCE

Human kind cannot bear very much reality.

T. S. Eliot 1888–1965, 'Burnt Norton'

ENERGY

Pent-up powers are gained by an ordered life.

Tubby Clayton 1885–1972

ENVY

The disease of men is this — that they neglect their own fields and go and weed the fields of others.

Mencius (Meng K'o) 372–289BC

Of health in others

I would give
All that I am to be as thou now art.

Percy Bysshe Shelley 1792–1822

ESSENTIALS

A godly, righteous and sober life.

Book of Common Prayer

It is very little that is necessary to make up the essentials of life.

Lord what we have not give us.
Lord what we know not teach us.
Lord what we are not make us.
Forgive what we have been.
Sanctify what we are.
And order what we shall be . . .   Amen

Traditional

EUCHARIST, The

Prayers beforehand

Every morning lean your arms awhile upon the window-sill of heaven and gaze upon the Lord.
  Then with the vision in your heart, turn strong to meet your day.

Anonymous

May the Lord grant us his peace and life eternal.

O God who in a wonderful sacrament has left us a memorial of your passion, help us so to venerate the sacred mysteries of your body and blood that we may perceive within ourselves the fruits of your redemption through Jesus Christ our Lord.   Amen.

Traditional

The importance of the eucharist*

The eucharist is *the* action by which God-in-Christ sanctifies us in the world. All our actions and thoughts are related to and flow from this thanksgiving celebration. Each time we participate fully we obey our Lord's command, and share completely with his universal Church as we, and Christians all down the ages, enter simultaneously, Christ's gift and dying on the Cross.

In so doing we are — like the bread — taken, blessed, broken and shared so that re-formed and strengthened we may become yet more lovingly agents for Christ, fulfilled in his service. The entire liturgy is presented by the use of outward signs which point to and flow from the hidden truth, that Christ is really present in the assembly itself, in ministry and word, in the celebrant** and more particularly the sacraments themselves.

* From the Greek word for thanksgiving; also called the Lord's Supper, the liturgy, the Mass, holy communion.

** Also called the president or officiant.

Cleanse my conscience, O God, by your Holy Spirit, that our Lord Jesus Christ when he comes to me in this holy sacrament may find in me a home prepared to welcome him.

Traditional

Be still to know God,
for only the silent hear.

Anima Christi

Soul of Christ sanctify me.
Body of Christ save me.
Blood of Christ refresh me.

Water from the side of Christ wash me.
Passion of Christ strengthen me.

O good Jesus hear me.
Within thy wounds hide me.
Suffer me not to be separated from thee.

From the malicious enemy defend me.
In the hour of death call me,
and bid me to come to thee;
that with thy saints
I may praise thee for all eternity.   *Traditional*

Prayers during communion

Be gentle when you touch bread
Let it not lie uncared for, unwanted.
So often bread is taken for granted.

There is so much beauty in bread
Beauty of rain and toil
Beauty of sun and soil
The winds of the air caressed it
Christ often blessed it
Be gentle when you touch bread.   *Author unknown*

Be loving when you drink wine
so freely received and joyfully shared
In the spirit of him who cared
Warm as a flowing river
Shining and clear as the sun
Deep as the soil
of human toil
The winds and the air caressed it
Christ often blessed it
Be loving when you drink wine.

Lord let my possessed life fall away that your selfless
life may soar in me. Help me to remember, when I
often forget, that with you I am no longer alone.

Then Lord, in your great patience, show me how to
serve you with a quiet mind, a joyful smile and a
loving heart.   Amen.

As watchmen look for the morning so do we look for
thee, O Christ. Come with the dawning of the day and
make thyself known to us in the breaking of the bread
for thou art our God for ever and ever. Amen.

Traditional

You fill up my senses
Like a night in the forest
Like a mountain in springtime
Like a walk in the rain
Like a storm in the desert
Like a sleepy blue ocean
  You fill up my senses
  come fill me again.

Come let me love you
Let me give my life to you
Let me drown in your laughter
Let me die in your arms
Let me lie down beside you
Let me always be with you
  Come let me love you
  come love me again.

John Denver, 'Annie' (adapted)

In the quietness of his bread
and the stillness of his wine
our fears are made no more
and our love is made divine.

In the prayerfulness of loving
and this sacrament begun
our brokenness is mended
and through gentleness made One.

Prayers after communion

I am renewed as light crosses life
Touched by his stillness and imbued with his strength
His peace in the bread; his joy in the wine;
For so much healing's in breaking

So much of the whole in the part
As seeds are to the loaf, grapes are to the vine;
So are we changing, growing, sharing,
This peace for our days, this joy for our years.

O Christ who holds the open gate,
O Christ who drives the furrow straight,
O Christ, the plough, O Christ, the laughter,
Of holy white birds flying after,
Lo, all my heart's field red and torn
And thou wilt bring the young green corn,
The young green corn divinely springing,
The corn that makes the holy bread
By which the soul of man is fed,
The holy bread, the food unpriced,
The everlasting mercy, Christ.

John Masefield 1874–1967

Just as the bread which we break
was scattered over the earth, was gathered in
and became one,
Bring us together from everywhere
Into the kingdom of your peace.

The Didache

EVENING

Thanksgiving

At the close of another day, we come to thee, O Lord.
We thank thee for all that has been good and happy
    in our work and leisure:
For all who have helped us by their kindness and
    example:
For all those whom, by thy grace, we have been
    enabled to help:
For lessons we have learnt through new experiences.

Traditional

Penitence

We ask thy forgiveness for any way in which we have
   failed thee or others during this day:
For the things we have said when we should have kept
   silent:
For the cowardice that prevented us from speaking
   when we should:
For the opportunities we missed through blindness or
   laziness.   *Traditional*

Intercession

We pray for all those who are in pain or distress this
   night:
For the homeless, the lonely, the fearful.
Use this our prayer on their behalf, that they may find
   the comfort of thy presence.
Bless all in this house, and all who need our prayers,
   and grant us thy peace through the hours of
   darkness.   *Traditional*

Grace

May God Almighty bless us with his Holy Spirit; for
the love of Jesus.   Amen.

EVIL

The threads that make up our human nature are two-
ended. There is no capacity for feeling pride without an
equal capacity for feeling shame. One cannot feel joy
unless one can also feel despair. We have no capacity
for good without an equal capacity for evil. What then
is evil, but the self seeking to fulfil its own secret
needs. All that is necessary is that we face it, and
choose.   *Chinese*

No man is justified in doing evil on the ground of
expediency.

                              Theodore Roosevelt 1858–1919

All that is necessary for the triumph of evil, is that the good men do nothing.

Edmund Burke 1729–1797

Deal with evil as if it were a sickness in yourself.

Shoo King

Be prepared.

Boy Scout motto

But evil is wrought by want of thought
  As well as want of heart.

Thomas Hood 1799–1845

Order is heaven's first law.

Alexander Pope 1688–1744

No one became thoroughly bad all at once.

Decimus Junius Juvenalis (Juvenal) 60–140

Make no mistake: 'Bad company is the ruin of good character'.

1 Corinthians 15:33 New English Bible

Once to every man and nation
  Comes the moment to decide
In the strife of truth and falsehood
  For the good or evil side.
And the choice goes by for ever
  'Twixt that darkness and that light.

James Russell Lowell 1819–1891

The true doctrine of omnipresence is, that God reappears with all his parts in every moss and cobweb. The value of the universe contrives to throw itself into every point. If the good is there, so is the evil; if the affinity, so the repulsion; if the force, so the limitation. Thus the universe is alive.

Ralph Waldo Emerson 1803–1882

He that will not apply new remedies must expect new evils; for time is the great innovator.

Sir Francis Bacon 1561–1626

EXCESS

Excess of sorrow laughs. Excess of joy weeps.

William Blake 1757–1827

EXCLUSION

He that shuts love out
in turn shall be shut out
from Love, and on her
threshold lie, howling
in the outer darkness.

Alfred, Lord Tennyson 1809–1892

EYES

Incline thine ear . . . open thine eyes and see.

Isaiah 37:17

The eye is the lamp of the body. If therefore your
eye is sound your whole body will be full of light.
But if your eye is evil, your body will be full of
darkness. If therefore the light in you is really
darkness, that is darkness indeed.

Matthew 6:22

Be very careful that your light never becomes darkness.

Luke 11:35

How can you say to your brother, 'Brother, let me take
out the speck that is in your eye' when you yourself do
not see the log that is in your own eye?

Luke 6:41

Their eyes were opened and they knew.

Luke 24:31

Keep my eyes open, and my imagination alert,
that I may see how things look to others,
especially the unwell, the worried, the over-worked.
For your love's sake.   Amen.

Rita Snowden

FAILURE

Lord, teach me now and every day that what the world
calls failure is of passing value. Teach me only to care
for that which brings me close to you.   Amen.

One moment of failure can be God's moment of grace.

FAIR-MINDEDNESS

Lord, it is comparatively easy to be fair-minded when
all is within my control, my interests and my concern.
But when the going is hard, there is the testing. Help
me then, especially when others use aggression instead
of love, to remain fair-minded and God-centred,
enabling me for your sake to think caringly and calmly,
to the benefit of all.   Amen.

I detest what you say but will defend to the death your
right to say it.

Voltaire 1694–1778

FAITH

No, the opposite of faith is not doubt. Doubt is an
important strand in the rope of faith. No, the opposite
of faith is fear, fear which paralyses and corrodes.

Ivor Smith-Cameron

FAMILY

Lord teach me every day how important it is to give
adequate time and thoughtfulness, care and lovingness
to my family.

My wife (husband) will only be truly my wife
(husband) if I help her (him) to be so, by anticipating

her (his) needs, so that with imagination and delight we may share our loads and achieve our hopes and dreams together.

My children will only feel and know my love, share my insights and benefit from my laughter and understanding if I spend time enough with them.

My parents will only discern my thankfulness and loving joy if I maintain links, and help when needed.

My friends and neighbours will only enjoy the fruits of care and concern, happiness and enthusiasm, if I extend to them the same qualities that are shared in my family.

And you, Lord, will only know that I love you if we meet every day and then I seek to acknowledge and share in my responsibilities as part of the family of man, through the example of your only son who took the pattern of the family into the pattern of discipleship and the world-wide fellowship of the Church, now and in all ages.   Amen.

Glory be to the Father
and to the Son
and to the Holy Spirit.   Amen

Heavenly Father thank you that
the Son of God became
the son of man
in order that
the family of man might become
the family of God.

Father, this is your great expectation:
make it also mine.

In the dark, Lord, there is no difference in the colour of
    skin.
In giving blood, Lord, there is no distinction in our
    human need.
In sleep, Lord, there is no separation in the peace you
    give.

In completing life there is no exception to the closing of
  years.
Then, Lord, help us to bridge the chasms of fear
  and to heal all that divides us from one
  another. Amen.

Ring in the valiant man and free,
  The larger heart, the kindlier hand;
  Ring out the darkness of the land,
Ring in the Christ that is to be.
          Alfred, Lord Tennyson 1809–1892, 'In Memoriam'

All happy families resemble one another; every
unhappy family is unhappy in its own way.
          Leo Tolstoy 1828-1910, Anna Karenina

FAR AWAY, For those

Father, who led men of wisdom by the shining of a star
and brought people to the promised land, guide and
protect all who are distant from land and far away from
home that they may know the power of your saving
presence and the nearness of your spirit, now and
always. Amen.

FEAR

Father, thank you for showing me in your son Jesus
that the only way to overcome fear is to risk going into
the world of fear and confront it. To go ever deeper
until I realise that the fear is of my own making, to
search out why, and do or accept something in order to
release myself from its power. Thank you for leading
me through darkness into light. Amen.

Beloved let us love one another: for love is of God . . .
Perfect love casts out fear.   *1 John 4:7, 18*

Fear creates the victim.

It is what people know about themselves inside that
makes them afraid.

I fear men, not God. He understands and forgives; they
do not.   *Nikos Kazantzakis 1883–1957*

Fear takes hold chiefly of the people who have few
interests beyond themselves.

Melville Harcourt 1909-1984

FEAR NOT
Through many dangers, toils and snares
I have already come;
'Tis grace hath brought me safe thus far,
And grace will lead me home.
John Newton 1725–1807

FEEBLENESS
Faith is weak, Lord,
Life is hard.

For some
there is constant pain,
for others
death comes too soon;
some escape from fear
by going out of their mind
or taking their lives.

Yet we can be glad
because there is so much courage in the world.

So much generosity,
personal kindness
self-sacrifice
love and hope.

Faith is weak,
life is hard
but Christ has died
and Christ is risen;
your Holy Spirit
is at work among us,

accomplishing more than we have ever thought to ask,
making us better men and women
than we ever thought to be,
making the world a brighter and more joyful place
than we could ever have imagined. *Alan Gaunt*

FEELINGS

Feelings are not endings, nor beginnings. They neither
sustain nor promise eternal life. But feelings are an
important gauge, Lord, and I am so grateful that you
can teach me the feeling of what is right and what is
wrong, when to say 'yes' and when to say 'no'. For
feelings must always be directed in obedience to your
love, Lord. Thank you for every feeling, now and
always. Amen.

FLOWER

All's in this flower

Times, seasons, losses, all the fruits of woe,
Beauty's fragility, and death's bare gain
Plucked in passing by, five minutes ago.

All's in this flower, the war of life and death,
God's character and purpose written down,
The face of love, the proof and power of faith
All's here, and all unknown. *Frank Kendon*

FOOD

Better beans and bacon in peace
Than cakes and ale in fear. *Anonymous*

I am the bread of life. He who comes to me shall never
hunger. *John 6:35*

Bread of heaven,
Feed me now and evermore.

William Williams 1717–1791

FORGIVENESS

> Lord, draw from our hearts the spring of forgiveness.
> Make your sunlight our own. In the spirit of Christ,
> help us to forgive others for being different;
> for not sharing our opinions;
> for loving others, but only liking us,
> or not liking us at all.
>
> Help us to forgive Christ for being so good,
> and all whom life visits with blessings
> greater than our own,
> and lesser than we would like.
>
> Help us to be forgiven by all who find us
> difficult, moody, overbearing or depressed.
> Help us to forgive ourselves and know ourselves
> forgiven by surrender to you.
> Forgive what we have been;
> establish what we shall become;
> and hold us in the strength of your love,
> given to us in Jesus Christ our Lord.   Amen.

Priest: Let God take away this bitterness.
Penitent: I will never forgive her (him).
Priest: You do not lose your peace over someone
           else's sin, but only over your own.

(After absolution)
Penitent: It was as if God brought a vacuum cleaner
          and sucked out all the bitterness of the years.
Larry Christenson (adapted)

When I act compulsively (for example, lose my temper
with my friend) nothing restores me to goodness and
love so effectively as his refusal to believe that the me
who lost my temper is anything but a superficial and
unimportant aspect of my full self. Without it, there can
be no forgiveness. All forgiveness, God's and man's,
must be rooted in truth.
H. A. Williams, b.1919, Soundings

Prayer asking God's forgiveness

Almighty God, our heavenly Father,
we have sinned against you and against our fellow
  beings,
in thought and word and deed,
and in what we have left undone.
We are truly sorry,
and repent of all our sins.
For the sake of your son Jesus Christ
who died for us,
forgive us all that is past;
and grant that we may serve you
in newness of life
to the glory of your name.   Amen.

Alternative Service Book 1980 (adapted)

Absolution

Almighty God, who forgives all who truly repent, have
mercy upon you, pardon and deliver you from all your
sins, confirm and strengthen you in all goodness, and
keep you in life eternal; through Jesus Christ our
Lord.   Amen.   *Alternative Service Book 1980*

Forgiveness brings release from a sense of guilt (and) a
new sense of joy and freedom.

Bernard Meland, The Realities of Faith

The inward witness, the assuring sense
Of an Eternal Good which overlies
The sorrow of the world, Love which outlives
All sin and wrong. Compassion which forgives
To the uttermost, and Justice whose clear eyes
Through lapse and failure to the intent
And judge our frailty by the life we meant.

John Greenleaf Whittier 1807–1892

Lord how often am I to forgive my brother if he goes
on wronging me? As many as seven times? Jesus

replied, 'I do not say seven times; I say seventy times
seven.'　　　　　　　*Matthew 18:21-22, New English Bible*

Her sins, which are many, are forgiven; for she loved
much.　　　　　　　　　*Luke 7:47, Authorised Version*

In nature everything has meaning. And everything is
forgiven. And it would be strange not to forgive.
　　　　　　　　　　　Anton Chekhov 1860–1904

Forgive us the sins of disunity, O Lord: pride and
jealousy and narrow mindedness. Forgive us the sins of
unity: lack of imagination, apathy and indifference.
Make us many in gifts and talents and vision.　Amen.
　　　　　　Simon H. Baynes, Prayers for Today's Church

FREEDOM

Freedom means you have nothing left to lose.

With freedom comes the burden of choice.

The disciplined life that is the only effective way to
durable freedom involves *firstly* the inner way to a
knowledge of God from whom all freedom comes. Then
comes the *second* part that concerns the individual life
of mind and body. All is consummated in the *third* part
which concentrates its work in relationships with other
people. Thus the life of spiritual discipline consists of
contemplation, ascetic living and purity of
relationships. First comes the love of God, then the
loving discipline of oneself, and finally service to our
neighbours, who, as Jesus reminds us in the parable of
the Good Samaritan, include everyone in immediate
relationship with us.
　　　　　　　　Martin Israel, The Spirit of Counsel

True liberty is liberty to do what we ought to do. It is
not the liberty to do as we like.
　　　　　　　　Field-Marshall Montgomery 1887–1976

FRIENDSHIP

A true friend
unburdens freely,
advises justly,
assists readily,
adventures boldly,
takes all patiently,
defends courageously,
and continues a friend
unchangeably.   *William Penn 1644–1718*

Friendliness is admirable, but it is not friendship.
                              F. L. Lucas 1894–1967

The only way to have a friend is to be one: if you want
to receive letters you have to write to friends first.

Old friends are best. King James used to call for his old
shoes; they were easiest for his feet.
                              John Selden 1584–1654

Those friends thou hast, and their adoption tried,
Grapple them to thy soul with hoops of steel.
                              William Shakespeare 1564–1616

When we meet with difficulties we think of our
relatives; but on the brink of danger we rely on our
friends.

                              Chinese aphorism

FRUSTRATION

Frustration, Lord, is my contribution to discontent in
the world. My wrongful response to all your gifts in
how *not* to live the day; my failure of imagination, trust
and love; my inability to manipulate your world or
accept it for all the rich variety it contains.
    Shake me up, Lord, and open my eyes afresh to the
beauty and wonder of your world and true life in and
through Christ Jesus our Lord.   Amen.

GENTLENESS

Lord, teach me how important it is to be gentle.

GIFTS (talents)

A person is what they do with their silence.

The real meaning of intercession is not telling God in one's own words of the needs and sorrows of the world, but through the silent attentive spirit focusing the love of God where the need is greatest.

GIVING

You give but little when you give of your possessions. It is when you give of yourself that you truly give.

Kahlil Gibran 1883–1931

I want to love you
without clutching,
appreciate you without judging,
join you without invading,
invite you without demanding,
leave you without guilt,
criticise you without blaming,
and help you without insulting.
If I can have the same
from you
then we can truly meet
and enrich each other.

Virginia Satir

Great gifts may be given by little hands.

I am not an island ... I am not a rock ... I am connected by a web of loving relationships to the people who have brightened my life ... they are God's gifts to me and I spread their names around me, as a child spreads out his birthday presents.

Damian Lundy, To Grow in Christ

Cleanse and inspire the Church that Christ the sower may scatter his seed to the world.

Guide and strengthen your Church, all followers of Christ, to work the rocky soil of our hearts. Help her clear the weeds and brambles of our contemporary society that the seed may grow and yield:
Lord hear us, Lord graciously hear us.

We pray for the land you sow that the nations may be guided by your word and may bear the fruits of love, joy, peace, humility, trustfulness; that nation may be reconciled to nation, believers to those who cannot believe, Christians to fellow Christians, husbands to wives, parents to children:
Lord hear us, Lord graciously hear us.

We pray for our local community, the streets we walk, the paths where the seed won't grow.
 Thank you Father for the signs of life, resurrected from the cold earth. The green blades of daffodils and crocus, the bare branches of lilac and forsythia now budding; the signs that the sower has been before us.
 We thank you for all our opportunities to grow and ask your guidance and direction.
 We pray for the fruits of Christian fellowship and co-operation with our neighbours.
 We pray for those who labour here and ask that their work may be to your glory.

Let us pray for all those seeds struggling in barren places, or amongst thorns and weeds.
 For all in trouble, suffering pain or loss.
 For the lonely, the ill, the distressed, the poor and the hungry. Help us to care and cultivate your garden.

We pray that our hearts may be a fertile soil for your word. Be with us that it may grow and prosper and bear abundant fruit.
 We thank you for the fullness of the eternal harvest.
 For all who have died in Christ, those who rest in his peace and rise in glory. Amen.   *Gavan Riley*

There is nothing so precious you can't give it away.
Melville Harcourt 1909-1984

Not what we have but what we share,
for the gift without the giver is bare.
Who gives himself with his arms feeds three,
himself, his hungry neighbour, and me.

Anonymous

Almighty God, fountain of all wisdom, who knowest
our necessities before we ask, and our ignorance in
asking, have pity on our infirmities, and grant that
those things which for our infirmities we dare not ask
and for our blindness we cannot ask, vouchsafe to give
us for the worthiness of they Son, our saviour, Jesus
Christ.   Amen.

Traditional

Giving changes a man's impulse to cruelty into
kindness of heart.
Nachman of Bratzlav 1772–1811

GOALS

Let us then live, speak, work and pray 'to the greater
glory of God'. This will afford us the same motive as
Christ our Lord had. This will direct all our work to an
end beyond ourselves. It will also strengthen us when
life seems to lack purpose and enable us to ask 'Whose
is the glory I am seeking, in the things I do and say?' It
will help us to see that we are *instruments only* in the
hand of our Lord.
Eric Symes Abbott 1906–1983

Do not act as if you had ten thousand years to throw
away. Be good for something while you live, and it is
in your power.
Marcus Aurelius 121–180

He who lives for others shall have great troubles, but they shall seem to him small.

He who lives for himself shall have small troubles, but they shall seem to him great.   *Anonymous*

See also Aim

GOD

O my God
If I worship thee in desire for heaven,
    exclude me from heaven;
If I worship thee for fear of hell
    burn me in hell.
But if I worship thee for thyself alone
then withhold not from me thine eternal beauty.
Rabia, a Muslim woman mystic of Basrah and Jerusalem c. 800

Design is manifest everywhere. Whether we be laymen or scientists we must postulate a Lord of the Universe, give him what shape you will.
                            Sir Arthur Keith 1866–1955

Speak to him then for he heareth;
Spirit and spirit can meet;
Closer is he than breathing;
Nearer than hands or feet.   *Anonymous*

GOODNESS

Goodness is something so simple: always to live for others, never to seek one's own advantage.
                            Dag Hammarskjöld 1905–1961

Goodness by itself can be a little dull; but saintliness goes beyond and takes supreme risks and dares all.

Good men smile; saints dare to laugh and generate the good humour that puts you at ease.

I believe ... the spirit of good that men crave will prove stronger than evil and fear.
                            Boris Pasternak 1890–1960

GOLDEN RULE, The

The Zoroastrian:	Do as you would be done by.
The Confucian:	What you do not wish done to yourself, do not do to others.
The Taoist:	Do unto others as you would have others do unto you.
The Jew:	Whatsoever you do not wish your neighbour to do to you, do not do unto him.
The Muslim:	Let none of you treat your brother in a way he himself would dislike to be treated.
The Christian:	Always treat others as you would like them to treat you.

GOOD SAMARITAN (Are you one?)

1 Do you walk by and pretend it's not there?
2 Are you one who injures or the one who heals?
3 Do you bind up the wounds at home, at work, in this community, or wherever you are?
4 Are you prepared to do the extra bit to ensure the healing remains healed?
5 Do you pay the price in time, care or money?
6 Do you come from the safe heights of your protected Jerusalem down to the heat and grime of the dust-road of real life?
7 Do you hug the bank and avoid the open road?
8 Are you a shade and refuge for others or the cause of their unrest and unease?
9 How far are you prepared to go to help and heal?
10 Are you able to prevent others being waylaid by the traps of life and assaults on their time, energy, attitudes and values?

GOSPEL, The

The gospel has two sides, the believing side and the living side.

Preacher in the Southern states of the USA

GOSSIP

A tart temper never mellows with age, and a sharp tongue is the only edged tool that grows keener with constant use.

Washington Irving 1783–1859, Rip Van Winkle

GRACE, The

The grace of our Lord Jesus Christ, and the love of God and the fellowship of the Holy Spirit be with us all evermore.   Amen.   *Traditional*

GRIEF

Jesus wept.
Thank heaven:
Then so can I.

GROWTH

The mind grows always by intercourse with a mind more than itself. That is the secret of all teaching.

Archbishop William Temple 1881–1944

If only I may grow firmer, simpler — quieter, warmer.

Dag Hammarskjöld 1905–1961

I had to continue growing. I would not be a crippled tree. Indeed it is suffering to go on growing, to hold to what is, to try to understand, to knock down one's preconceptions. To find one's memories ravaged by time, one's intimate illusions ripped up, laughter for one's own private desolation the only answer; to realise how difficult, agonising, is the process of understanding, and how long it takes.

Han Suyin, The Crippled Tree

GRUMBLING

> Simon: Master, I did grumble, and I'm very sorry.
>
> Jesus: Did you? Well now, listen. There was a man with two sons, and he told them to go and work on his allotment. And one of them said, cheerfully, 'Yes, rather, Dad.' But he met some friends and forgot all about it and never did a stroke. The other son said, 'No, I won't go. I hate digging.' But afterwards he thought, 'Oh well, I suppose I'd better,' and went off grumbling and did as he was told. Now which of those two did the will of his father?
>
> *Dorothy L. Sayers 1893–1957*, The Man Born to be King

HANDICAP (child)

Little blind girl
loved at 3
What will your future be?

Little deaf boy
loathed at 4
here you stay behind your door.

Little fair girl
loved at 5
without a lung and still alive.

Little brown boy
loathed at 6
don't imagine races mix.

Little black girl
loved at 7
rickets mar your way to heaven.

Little dumb boy
loathed at 8
what will be your silent fate?

Little lame girl
loved at 9
what will be your anodyne?

Crippled pale boy
loathed at 10
will you ever walk again?

Such signs without
need love within;
all the difference
is not in skin.

It is the *difference*
we despise.
That is only caused
by our different eyes
that see yet do not see
that accepted signs
are love's surprise.

HANDS

Lord your hands clasp my hands
and fold my life in two;
Lord your eyes hold my gaze
and warm my whole life through;
Lord your words touch my mind
and focus all in you.

Those who use their hands creatively are invariably
contented.

Put your hand in the hand of the man
who stilled the waters;
Put your hand in the hand of the man
who calmed the sea.

Gene MacLellan

O God take the skill that resides in my hand and use it
today.

Rita Snowden

Christ has no hands but our hands
  to do his work today;

Christ has no feet but our feet
  to lead us in his way;
Christ has no lips but our lips
  to tell men why he died;
Christ has no love but our love
  to win men to his side.

Anonymous

Lord, hold my hand
  I so need your living kindness;
Lord, hold my hand
  All through life, in joy and grief;
Lord, hold my hand
  When I'm sick with fear and anxious;
Lord, hold my hand
  In the wonder of relief.
Lord, hold my hand
  When it's dark and storms are raging;
Lord, hold my hand
  And help me live it through.
Lord, hold my hand
  When I'm lifted, joyful, loving;
Lord, hold my hand
  When I'm trying something new.
Lord, hold my hand
  When I fail or faint or waver;
Lord, hold my hand
  For I know your love is true.
Lord, hold my hand
  When I'm lonely, weary, ageing;
Lord, hold my hand
  When there's only me — and you.   *Anonymous*

O Lord take my ears and hear through them,
take my hands and use them,
take my lips and speak through them,
take my eyes and smile through them,
take my heart and mind and will,

and use them as lamps of love,
by which your light may shine in all
the darkness of this suffering world.

Anonymous

HAPPINESS

We have no more right to consume happiness without
producing it than to consume wealth without
producing it.

George Bernard Shaw 1856–1950

Men always return to the place where they are most
happy. *Lettie Harcourt*

Happiness is like coke, something you get in the
process of producing something else.

Aldous Huxley 1894–1963

There is no duty we so much underrate as the duty of
being happy.

Robert Louis Stevenson 1850–1894, 'An Apology for Idlers'

Happiness is found on the familiar highways of life;
contentment is a herb that grows very close to the
earth. *Melville Harcourt 1909-1984*

How happy are the humble-minded, for the kingdom
of heaven is theirs.

How happy are those who know what sorrow means,
for they will be given courage and comfort.

Happy are those who claim nothing, for the whole
earth will belong to them.

Happy are those who are hungry and thirsty for
goodness, for they will be fully satisfied.

Happy are the merciful, for they will have mercy
shown to them.

Happy are the utterly sincere, for they will see God.

Happy are those who make peace, for they will be

known as the sons of God.

Happy are those who have suffered persecution for the cause of goodness, for the kingdom of heaven is theirs.

And what happiness will be yours when people blame you and ill-treat you and say all kinds of slanderous things against you for my sake! Be glad then, yes, be tremendously glad — for your reward in heaven is magnificent.

They persecuted the prophets before your time in exactly the same way.   *Matthew 5:3-11*

HATE

The game of hate-trading usually ends the moment one party refuses to play.   *Earl Jabay,* The God Players

The seeds of hatred always destroy themselves.

Time is running out, put hatred to sleep.
                                        Shin Shalom b. 1904

Now hatred is by far the longest pleasure;
Men love in haste, but they detest at leisure.
                    George Gordon Noel, Lord Byron 1788–1824

If you hate your son, accustom him to luxuries.
                                        Chinese aphorism

HAVING

The African is; the European has.   *Anonymous*

Father, I cannot help thinking that some children have so many things there is nothing to strive for, no initiative that can be taken, nothing left to hope for.

Other children have so little, and therefore must make the best with what they are.

As one of your eternal children, help me to value daily the things you give me, and the qualities within me that you wish to grow.   Amen.

HEADACHE

The pressure in my head is unrelenting, Lord, like the
incessant beat of an angry drum. Through this
throbbing I remember that your head too was torn with
pain, and deeply wounded. Give me your strength and
perseverance, Lord, and by your wounds heal the roots
of my aching.

HEALING

In Christ
Healing brings relaxation,
release from captivity,
freedom.
Therefore seek healing
In Christ.

Lord
help me each and every day
fearlessly to question
generously to give
lovingly to offer
the truth of help,
And in that offering
to enable others
to smile,
to relax,
to see,
to grow,
to flourish;
For in you
I give to them
the commitment
of a life
of friendship.

Take from me all that hinders the work of your healing
power, all our sins, our anxieties and fears, all
resentment and hardness of heart, and help us to learn
to enter into stillness and peace with you and to know
that you are our healer and redeemer.   Amen.

Brother Joseph

Lord, the outer symptoms of my illness may be hiding
a fundamental sin, something so deep and established
that it affects the whole of my attitude.
    Cleanse me through and through from my secret
faults and my hidden fears.   Amen.

HEALTH

Lord, help me to be grateful for the release of surplus
matter and ease to my body and mind.
    Make me aware of the fact that a well-ordered body
aids a well-ordered life.
    Help me to eat and to exercise wisely and well,
through Jesus Christ our Lord.   Amen.

Lord, help me in this time of difficulty, and where
there are medicines to be taken, enable me to
understand that these are for my eventual health, and
health is the wonderful gift that you give to enhance
the welfare of your kingdom.   Amen.

The truth is that people who worship health cannot
remain healthy.

G. K. Chesterton 1874–1936

Lord, as you went into the wilderness for a long time,
strengthen me in confronting the mysteries
of disciplined eating.
Let me take only what I need,
and not all I desire.
Let my will overcome the temptations

of my own and others' encouragement
to have a little more.
Keep me from tetchiness and imagined meals;
Let me be watchful of headaches
and mindful of drinking sensibly and enough.
And what you take from my body give in strength
to my mind, my will, and my spirit, for Jesus's
    sake.   Amen.

Lord teach me how important it is to regulate my
health through sensible eating, balanced diets and
regular exercise. Healthy bowels are an index to the
enjoyment of full life, clear skin, lack of headaches, and
general well being. Thank you for such possibilities
each and every day.   Amen.

Your first duty in helping others is, if possible, to
preserve your health.

David Chapman

The remedy is worse than the disease.

Sir Francis Bacon 1561–1626

The health of body and mind are related.

Chinese aphorism

God be merciful unto us and bless us.
That thy way may be known upon earth:
Thy saving health among all nations.

Psalm 67:1-2

HEART

A good heart breaks bad luck.

Miguel de Cervantes 1547–1616,
Sancho Panza in Don Quixote

Beat the drum,
   Turn on the news,
      They've done it at last.
         Swapped a heart.
Taken that living organ of life from one body to
   another.
O teach us from this man-made miracle, Lord
That we all need new hearts,
Hearts of understanding
   Compassion,
      Tolerance and love.
Loosen our fears of colour, and race,
and show us again in this scientific wonder,
our common heritage.
And so, Father, awaken and renew your spirit
within me, and perfect this with open joy,
through Jesus Christ our Lord.   Amen.

Roger Bush

HEAVEN

And soul by soul and silently
her shining bounds increase,
and her ways are ways of gentleness
and all her paths are peace.

Sir Cecil Spring-Rice 1859–1918

Father, you are holy indeed and all creation rightly
gives you praise. All life, all holiness comes from you.

Eucharistic Prayer II, Roman Missal

From age to age you gather a people to yourself so that
from east to west a perfect offering may be made to the
glory of your name.

Eucharistic Prayer II, Roman Missal

HELL

Long is the way
And hard, that out of hell leads up to light.

John Milton 1608–1674

HELP

When I was a boy I fell into a hole in the ground and I was broken and could not climb out.

I might have died there: but a stranger came along and saved me. He said it was his obligation that, for help he had once received, he must, in return, help ten others; so that good deeds would spread out like the ripples from a pebble in a pond. I was one of his ten, and you became one of mine. And now I pass this obligation on to you.

Chinese

Help me to need no aid from men
that I may help such men as need.

Rudyard Kipling 1865–1936

. . . What in me is dark
Illumine, what is low raise and support.

John Milton 1608–1674, 'Paradise Lost'

HELPLESSNESS

The darkness deepens; Lord, with me abide:
When other helpers fail, and comforts flee,
Help of the helpless, O abide with me.

Henry Francis Lyte 1793–1847

I am weak, but thou art mighty;
Hold me with thy powerful hand.

William Williams 1719–1791

Almighty Father, king of kings, the lover of the meek,
Make me a friend of helpless things, defender of the
  weak.

E. Brailsford

HOLDING ON

Jesus judges by his presence, like a plumb-line to a wall. Just by the line's being there the wall knows whether or not it is straight.

Christianity is a religion of becoming.

Lord help me
to hold on in the pain
in the silence
in the nothing
of waiting . . .
with *you*.

HOLINESS

In our era, the road to holiness necessarily passes
through the world of action.

Dag Hammarskjöld 1905–1961

Sanctity cannot be achieved by proxy.

Melville Harcourt 1909-1984

HOLY SPIRIT

Spirit of the living God
fall afresh on me.
Break me, melt me,
mould me, fill me.
Spirit of the living God
fall afresh on me.

Daniel Iverson

HOME

Your home should be a place of quiet and happiness,
where no harsh word is ever heard, but love,
friendship, modesty, and a spirit of gentleness and
reverence rules all the time. But this spirit must not end
with the home.

Rabbi Joel Ben Abraham Shemariah

The most influential of all educational factors is the
conversation in a child's home.

Archbishop William Temple 1881–1944

We ask his blessing on this home and all who live in it.
May its doors be open to those in need and its rooms
filled with kindness. May love dwell within its walls,
and joy shine from its windows. May his peace protect
it and his presence never leave it.

Forms of Prayer for Jewish Worship

Let your blessing be on our home
that your peace may dwell here.
Let it be a place of welcome
that its happiness may be freely shared.

The Methodist marriage service (adapted)

HOMELESSNESS

Lord of the fields and the wayside, the desert, the
mountains and the city streets; Lord of the homeless,
the destitute and the outcast; Lord of the vagrants, the
desperate, the unloved; be a strength, a support and
courage to all who must wander without rest and have
no place to call their own.

You, who had nowhere to lay your head, guard and
guide your homeless people, this night (day) and
always.   Amen.

HOPE

Now is not the only time, Father, and however bad this
time may seem, illumine my feeble sight to see
opportunities for your work and your love to prevail.
First, let me pause, weigh and consider what your son
would do.   Amen.

O God our help in ages past,
Our hope for years to come.

Isaac Watts 1674–1748

The power of God is capable of finding hope where hope no longer exists, and a way where the way is impossible.

Gregory of Nyssa 330–395

Hope is not the closing of our eyes to difficulty, the risk of failures; it is a trust that if I fail now I shall not fail forever, that if I am hurt, I shall be healed — that life is good and love is powerful, that I shall find myself and others and God.

Padovano

Hope is one of your best gifts to us
Teach us to give it to others.   *Anonymous*

The gospel is a gospel of fulfilment. To travel hopefully is a better thing than to arrive.

Robert Louis Stevenson 1850–1894

Christ is the disturber, but where he disturbs he also inspires hope.
     There is always crisis where Christ is.

Gordon Davies

HOPELESSNESS

As one door closes another opens but only when the door is closed.
     Sometimes only the ending or death of an experience will bring about the birth of fresh opportunities bright with hope.

There is no place so deep
that he is not deeper.

Corrie Ten Boom 1892–1983

Where all else fails, there is the garden, the park or the quietness of water and the song of the bird.

HOSPITAL

Going to or leaving

The Lord himself is thy keeper;
The Lord is thy defence upon thy right hand;
The Lord shall preserve thee from all evil;
Yea it is even he that shall keep thy soul.
The Lord shall preserve thy going out, and thy coming
  in,
From this time forth for evermore.

Psalm 121:5-8

Doctor's prayer

Lord, may I be clean, polite, pleasant, truthful and understanding. Let me never be pompous or rude, but kind and considerate to nurses and patients and visitors, for they too have burdens to bear and needs which I can supply. Amen.

Nurse's prayer

Lord, help me to remain clean, cheerful, caring and alert to doctors' and patients' needs, and those who come to visit. In the strength which you alone can give, let me be quiet when I feel frayed, and gentle rather than rude, in the name of him who came to serve, even Jesus Christ our Lord. Amen.

Patient's prayer

Help me in a busy day for the doctors and nurses, to remember Lord that I am not the only patient, to trust in you, to follow medical instructions and, wherever possible, cheer up other patients and lend a hand. When people visit, help me gently but firmly to say when I am tired and to thank visitors for coming. Amen.

Father, thank you for the care and kindness of nurses who in patience, friendliness, and consideration give to each person the healing spirit of your son, that great physician of the soul, Jesus Christ our Lord. Amen.

Priest's prayer

Lord Jesus Christ, Son of the living God, be with me as
I visit those whom you love. Help me to find you in
them. Let my thoughts and words, my care and
gentleness, be your gift of peace and calm. Give me
your confidence which is searching love, through your
powers to heal and make whole. Amen.

Help me as I visit, Lord, to be clean, relaxed and tidy.
Enable me to be gentle, sympathetic and warm, though
never pushy or rude. Help me to be the bearer of
peacefulness, and the repository of stillness.

   Let me never be afraid of silence, and guide me to
speak about illness and about God naturally (which
means not endlessly). Let me find the natural and
easeful way of offering the prayers and sacraments and
blessing which you would give. Help me to leave
pleasantly and ask if there is anything that the patient
needs. Lord in the strength and power of your most
holy name, I offer this prayer. Amen.

Visitor's prayer

Thank you, Lord, for showing in the doctors and
nurses, that being clean and tidy, sympathetic, quiet
and cheerful, there is a mark of sensitivity and care
about the person I am visiting.

   Let me remember that I am not visiting to entertain
or instruct, but to reveal your love.

   Help me to remember that a short visit is
appreciated, rather than a long one, and that some
imaginative gift that meets their particular need is most
welcome. Before going let me ask if there is anything
needed, and leave cheerfully.

   In all I say or do not say, let me remember you are
there and that we share your presence, your love and
your most personal concern in the spirit of Jesus Christ
our Lord. Amen.

Lord, help me to remember the joy that comes from
'please' and 'thank you'.

Before an operation

Give to the winds thy fears;
hope, and be undismayed;
God hears thy sighs and counts thy tears;
God shall lift up thy head.

P. Gerhardt 1607–1676, tr. John Wesley

Trust in the Lord with all your heart. Never rely on
what you think you know.

Proverbs 3:5 Good News Bible

Afterwards

Praise the Lord, O my soul: and all that is within me
   praise his holy name.
Praise the Lord, O my soul: and forget not all his
   benefits.
He pardons all my guilt
and heals all my suffering.
He rescues me from deepest death
and surrounds me with constant love and tender
   affection;
he contents me.

Psalm 103:1-5, Book of Common Prayer and New English
Bible

They also serve who only stand and wait.

John Milton 1608–1674, 'On His Blindness'

Holding on — release

It happens as with cages: the birds outside despair to
get in, and those inside despair of getting out.

Michel Eyquem Montaigne 1533–1592

Food

Cauliflower is nothing but cabbage with a college
education.

Mark Twain 1835–1910

Thank you, Lord, for those who organise and prepare hospital meals. Let whatever is given be relative to the need, and all be served and received with consideration, with thankfulness and grace, through Jesus Christ our Lord.   Amen.

Full o' beans and benevolence.
Robert Smith Surtees 1803–1864

You blocks, you stones.   (*Julius Caesar*)

All hell shall stir for this.   (*Henry V*)

. . . crammn'd with distressful bread. [of sausages]
(*Henry V*)
William Shakespeare 1564–1616

HOSPITALITY

Greet and welcome each person as if (s)he were Christ in disguise; then discover Christ in them (*see* Hebrews 13:2).

HOT WEATHER

Father, when it is hot and not just warm, I become bad-tempered and irritable. The tension inside becomes like compressed steam.

Help me at such times to remember you and the cool confidence of your peace and the quietening of your ways, in the spirit of your blessed son Jesus Christ, our Lord.   Amen.

HOUSING ESTATE, On a

As they put the buildings up
They break the people down;
They take away
Our use of hands and legs.
And all we ever do
Who live here far from town
Is wait and wait and wait
As discarded human dregs.

HUMANITY

The spirit should not dominate the flesh and the heart
— it should unite them.

Michel Quoist

HUMOUR

I have been trying for a long time to understand God.
Now I have made friends with him. To love him truly
you must love change, and you must love a joke, these
being the true inclinations of his own heart.

Isaak Dinesen 1885–1962

Humour, that most saving grace.

Lord grant me a sense of humour in all things,
especially in what is said about me.
   Let the gift of your humour ease my tension, so that
healing may come and hours of worry become
moments of ease.

HUNGER

Lord, when I am hungry
   give me someone to feed,
When I am thirsty
   give water for their thirst.
When I am sad
   someone to lift from sorrow,
When burdens weigh upon me
   lay upon my shoulders
   the burden of my fellows,
Lord, when I stand
   greatly in need of tenderness,
   give me someone who yearns
   for love.
May your will be my bread,
your grace my strength,
your love my resting place.

Translation from a French prayer

These two parties still divide the world
Of those that have and those that want.

Alfred, Lord Tennyson 1809–1892

Eating bread from a newspaper
Drinking water from a chained cup.

Dylan Thomas 1914–1953, 'The Hunchback in the Park'

HYPOCRISY

No man is a hypocrite in his pleasures.

Samuel Johnson 1709–1784

ILLNESS

In everything from irritability and churlishness, to
harm, injury and misfortune, there is illness.

But why, Lord, why? What is the root? And what can
be done to put it right?

Help me to do my share in alleviating whatever I can,
beginning with this moment.   Amen.

Very sick

Lord we bring before you N who is very sick. In our
love and deep concern we offer all his (her) needs to
you. If he (she) be raised to new health, then
strengthen the way. If he (she) be raised to new life
beyond, let it be so. But whatever happens, let it be for
your glory and the furtherance of your kingdom, for the
sake of him who healed, restored, and forgave, Jesus
Christ our Lord.   Amen.

In this moment of great sickness be with N, Lord, and
support him (her) with your soothing hand and
abiding care. Let your love be seen and known through
the ministrations of doctors and nurses and all who
watch over N in his (her) time of need. For Jesus
Christ's sake.   Amen.

Be our strength in hours of weakness,
    in our wanderings be our guide;
Through endeavour, failure, danger,
    Father, be thou at our side.

L. M. Willis 1824–1908

IMPATIENCE

Those who are at peace with God pray and act without haste.

INDIFFERENCE

When Jesus came to Birmingham they simply passed
    him by,
They never hurt a hair of him, they only let him die;
For men had grown more tender, and they would not
    give him pain,
They only just passed down the street, and left him in
    the rain.

Still Jesus cried, 'Forgive them, for they know not what
    they do',
And still it rained the wintry rain that drenched him
    through and through.
The crowds went home and left the streets without a
    soul to see,
And Jesus crouched against a wall and cried for
    Calvary.

G. A. Studdert Kennedy 1883–1929, The Unutterable Beauty

INDISCRETION

O Lord, forgive me for doing this and help me to do better next time, for the glory of thy holy name and the salvation of my soul.

Fr. Kirik, elder of Mount Athos 1936

INDISPENSABILITY

Sometime, when you're feeling important,
  Sometime, when your ego's in bloom,
Sometime when you take it for granted
  You're the best qualified in the room;
Sometime when you feel that your going
  would leave an unfillable hole
Just follow this simple instruction
  And see how it *humbles* your soul.

Take a bucket and fill it with water
  Put your hand in it up to your wrist;
Pull it out, and the hole that's remaining
  Is the measure of how you'll be missed.

You may splash all you please when you enter;
  You can stir up the water galore;
But stop, and you'll find in a minute
  That it looks quite the same as before.

The moral in this quaint example
  Is to do just the best that you can.
Be proud of yourself, but remember,
  There's no indispensable man.

Anonymous

INFERIORITY

Lord, thank you for showing me that with you there is
no need for feelings of inferiority. For whatever I
cannot do, is left free to be completed by you in your
time and your way.   Amen.

Thank you, Lord, for showing me that apart from you,
no one is completely right
and I am not completely wrong.

Lord, with you there is no need to feel inferior to any
man. Strength wanes, weakness varies but you alone
remain strong and true.   Amen.

INFERTILITY

Lord it is so hard to accept. Some people love children
in an over-protective way. Others scarcely seem to care.
All I know is this instinct is deep within me, and I
would like to have his (her) child, our child, to
complete our love. But if that is not to be, help me to
cherish what we have.   Amen.

INFIRMITY

It is enough for me
Not to be doing, but to be!
I hear the wind among the trees,
Playing celestial symphonies;
I see the branches downward bent,
Like the keys of some great instrument.
And over me unrolls on high,
The splendid scenery of the sky.

Henry Wadsworth Longfellow 1807–1882

INFLEXIBILITY

The man who never alters his opinion is like standing
water, and breeds reptiles of the mind.

William Blake 1757–1827

Lord, help me to see
the wisdom of the tree.
Instruct me on when to yield
and when to stand firm.
The earth and the light
the wind and the rain
are nourishing, enabling,
strengthening, cleansing,
forces from outside
to strengthen me inside.
The orchestra of leaves;
the trade-route branches;
the silence from within
to give beauty without;

the infinite variety of the whole
the strong roots of attachment
the seeds of renewal
contained in winter
and spring's gentleness
for summer's joy.
All these and more
force me to ask,
Lord, help me to see
the wisdom of the tree.

It is not important who says sorry; but it is vital that
someone says sorry.

INJECTION

An injection is the medical sacrament that corresponds
to baptism.   *Anonymous*

Help me to accept that small pain is a little price to pay
for such a wonderful gift as healing.

INJURY

He who injures others injures himself.

Chinese aphorism

INSECURITY

In thee, O Lord, have I put my trust: let me never be
  put to confusion, deliver me in thy righteousness.
Bow down thine ear to me: make haste to deliver me.
And be thou my strong rock, and house of defence:
  that thou mayest save me.
For thou art my strong rock, and my castle: be thou
  also my guide, and lead me for thy name's sake.
Draw me out of the net, that they have laid privily for
  me: for thou art my strength.
Into thy hands, I commend my spirit: for thou hast
  redeemed me, O Lord, thou God of truth.

Psalm 31: 1-6, Coverdale

INSENSITIVITY

Lord I did not perceive the possibilities for your kingdom in that situation. I am deeply sorry. To show that my regret is sincere, I ask you to keep me vigilant for the next occasion and all opportunities that follow, for the sake of your son who was ever-sensitive, even Jesus Christ our Lord.   Amen.

INSIGHT

In all our deliberations may we perceive you in our midst, through Christ our Lord.   Amen.

What a man knows at fifty that he did not know at twenty boils down to something like this: the knowledge that he has acquired with age is not the knowledge of formulas, or forms of words, but of people, places, actions — a knowledge not gained by words but by touch, sight, sound, victories, failures, sleeplessness, devotion, love: in other words, the human experiences and emotions of this earth. And, perhaps, too, a little faith and a little reverence for the things you cannot see.   *Adlai Stevenson 1900–1965*

INSUFFICIENCY

Seek first the kingdom of God and his righteousness and you will be given everything that is necessary. So do not worry about the future. That will take care of itself. Each day has sufficient concerns of its own.
                              Matthew 6:33-34

INTENSITY

If I am intense, Lord, it is because I have lost a measure of trust, in you and in others, to help put things right.
    If I am intense, Lord, it is because I have lost a measure of prayer, and the calmness that comes from being with you.
    If I am intense, Lord, it is because I want to control the results of life, and steal from your glory.

Lord, intensity is me, but trustfulness is you.

Help me to be more trusting, and so more like you, for Jesus Christ's sake.   Amen.

ITCHING

Lord, I am tempted to ask you to let me start from scratch. But seriously, this itching is terrible, and I am helpless over such a little, seemingly invisible and terrible antagonist. You have given me will-power (and medicines to use). Help me to trust fully in your strengthening and sustaining as a way through this torment.   Amen.

JEALOUSY (child's)

Lord, his jealousy is as savage and tyrannical as fear. His will is a steel clamp; his ego as large as a man is big. Impotent and fearful he roars. He feels excluded, penned in, virile; yet uncontrolled and thwarted. He thinks none knows his needs sharpened on frayed parental nerves.

I know his fear, his exclusion and rage; I know.

I know, thank God, that he will grow and can learn to train the body for the man. And one day he may have a child, full of anger and destruction, yes, but tamed by the love that he has received from me.

Why be jealous because I am kind?
                    Matthew 20:15, New English Bible

JESUS PRAYER, The

[1] Lord Jesus Christ
[2] Son of the living God
[1] have mercy upon me
[2] a sinner.   *Traditional*

This prayer may be repeated over and over, like a mantra. When you breathe in[1], think of it as the Spirit cleansing you and inspiring you for love. When you breathe out[2], think that you are consciously expelling all that is impure.

JOB

The way you work at your job sheds darkness or light.
Every minute the choice is yours.

Father, thank you for giving me the ability to do my
job well, honestly and to the best of my ability.
    If I fail to maintain good standards help me to
remember all who would be glad to be in my place and
would work well. And when I do work hard and excel,
let me recall that without the gifts I have been given by
you I would be nothing.
    Thank you Father for the gift of my job; help me to
turn all I do to glory for you.   Amen.

Father, my job is not just work. It gives me contact
with others, discipline, interest, incentive, challenge
and response. The rough corners in me are rubbed off
by others. Their thoughts, their values, their capacities
tell me continually of a perspective other than my own.
    And you, who are creator of all, show me that all
work and all life should be lived in thankfulness to
you. Thank you, Father, thank you.   Amen.

JOBLESSNESS

As we enjoy our jobs today, we would not forget those
    who have none;
those who have no expectation of suitable work;
those who are worried because of family needs;
those finding their strength overtaxed;
those waiting long for advancement or reward;
those entering upon retirement and the loss of life-long
    interests;
those frail and old, and on the brink of the new
    life.   Amen.   *Rita Snowden*

Remember all who are unemployed and unemployable,
old and young, those recently made redundant and
those seldom if ever employed.

JOURNEYS

The longest journey is the journey within.

Dag Hammarskjöld 1905–1961

Beatitudes from an old person

Blessed are they who understand
my faltering steps and my palsied hand.

Blessed are they who know my ears today
must strain to catch the things they say.

Blessed are they who seem to know
that my eyes are dim and my wits are slow.

Blessed are they who looked away
when coffee spilled at the table today.

Blessed are they who never say,
'You've told that story twice today'.

Blessed are they who know the way
to bring back memories of yesterday.

Blessed are they who make it known
I'm loved, respected, not alone.

Blessed are they who know I'm at a loss
to find the strength to carry the cross.

Blessed are they who ease the days
on my journey home in loving ways.

Anonymous

Travelling

I read in a book
that a man called
Christ
went about doing good.
It is very disconcerting
that I am so easily
satisfied with
just going about.

Toyohiko Kagawa 1888–1960

To those who are travelling, good Lord, give a fair journey, whether by air, or land or sea, by river, lake or road.

Go with them in the way, to give them back to their own people in happiness and health.

Karachi prayer

Away from home
Ships and boats depart and arrive, planes and trains arrive and depart, cars and bicycles come and go. People leave for work and holidays and arrive home wearied or refreshed. So much of life journeys to arrive.

Now it is my turn; just my turn. Help me to trust in you Lord who help so many, to travel with you, calmly, quietly, holding your hand which reassures me of the knowledge that underneath are the everlasting arms.   Amen.

O Jesus
be the canoe that holds me in the sea of life,
be the steer that keeps me on the straight road.
Be the outrigger that supports me in times of great
    temptation.
Let thy spirit be my sail that carries me through each
    day.
Keep my body strong
so that I can paddle steadfastly on,
in the long voyage of life.

A New Hebridean prayer

It is not revolutions and upheavals
That clear the road to new and better days,
But revelations, lavishness and torments
Or someone's soul, inspired and ablaze.

Boris Pasternak 1890–1960

See also Hospital

JOY

Brighten up the world.

The Dammapada

There is no such thing as the pursuit of happiness;
there is only the discovery of joy.

Joyce Grenfell 1910–1979

JUDGING

Judge things as they really are, and not as they appear.

Miguel de Cervantes 1547–1616, Don Quixote

Wait like him
to judge like him
without passing judgement.
In his hand,
every moment has its meaning, its greatness,
its glory, its peace, its co-inherence.

Dag Hammarskjöld 1905–1961

KILLING

Reverence for life says never kill a moth or crush a
flower without first of all greeting the divine principle
within it.

Melville Harcourt 1909-1984

Yet each man kills the thing he loves,
By each let this be heard,
Some do it with a bitter look,
Some with a flattering word.
The coward does it with a kiss,
The brave man with a sword . . .

Ah! happy they whose hearts can break
   and peace of pardon win!
How else may man make straight his plan
   and cleanse his soul from sin?
How else but through a broken heart
   my Lord Christ enter in?

Oscar Wilde 1854–1900

You shall not murder.

Exodus 20:13; Deuteronomy 5:17

Who kills a man kills a reasonable creature, God's image; but he who destroys a good book, kills reason itself, kills the image of God, as it were in the eye.

John Milton 1608–1674, 'Areopagitica'

KINDNESS

A few kind words do not enter so deeply into a man as an established reputation for kindness.

Mencius (Meng-K'o) 372–289BC

There's more in the beauty of a smile than laughter can convey.

This England, Summer 1984

. . . that best portion of a good man's life;
His little, nameless, unremembered acts
Of kindness and of love.

William Wordsworth 1770–1850,
'Lines composed a few miles above Tintern Abbey'

The love of Christ is no more clearly shown than in a consistent will to be kind.

Little deeds of kindness, little words of love,
Help to make earth happy, like the heaven above.

Julia Carney 1823–1908, 'Little Things'

Have you had a kindness shown?
Pass it on!
'Twas not given for thee alone,
Pass it on!
Let it travel down the years,
Let it wipe another's tears,
Till in heaven the dead appears —
Pass it on!

Henry Burton

Question not, but live and labour
Till your goal be won,
Helping every feeble neighbour
Seeking help from none.
Life is mostly froth and bubble,
Two things stand like stone,
Kindness in another's trouble,
Courage in your own.

  Adam Lindsay Gordon 1833–1870, 'Ye Wearie Wayfarer'

Thanks be to the Lord:
For he hath showed me marvellous great kindness.

  Psalm 31:21

LAUGHTER

Lord who entered into our common daily life, increase
in us the grace to laugh generously with others and to
be ready to laugh at ourselves.

Save us from all 'holier than thou' attitudes, from
false pity, from self pity, and from being dull and
ponderous. Give to us in abundance the gifts of
joyfulness, kindliness and good humour.

We ask this for your name's sake.   Amen.

It is the heart that is not yet sure of its God that is
afraid to laugh in his presence.

Laughter is a property in man essential to his reason.

  Lewis Carroll 1832–1898

Like praying, a family that laughs together stays
together.

LEARNING

If I were travelling with two companions, one virtuous
and the other evil, both would be my masters. I would
examine what the first had that was good, and I would

imitate it; I would try to correct in myself the faults I
saw in the other.

Mencius (Meng-K'o) 372–289BC

From experience

Lord, thank you for my recent experience. Help me to
learn deeply from what has happened, to turn every
thought and every understanding into something good
and joyful, however long that may be.

Let my thanks be expressed in kindness and loving
appreciation, through Jesus Christ our Lord.   Amen.

Sticking to lessons learnt

Father, it is so easy, as time aids forgetfulness, to let
valuable lessons slide away, and areas of growth
become points of decay. Help me to hold firm to the
lessons I have learnt so that all my learning may
trustfully and lovingly be done in your name, through
him who persevered, even Jesus Christ our
Lord.   Amen.

LEAVING (home)

When time has passed and you must leave,
With love I hope you'll go,
Returning once again to me
With love, just as before.   *Moira A. Nicholls*

Letting go

When Alice climbed through the drawing-room mirror
into the looking-glass house it was to find herself in a
land of inverse perspective; everything was the wrong
way round, and each attempt to reach the distant hill at
the end of the garden path failed to bring it nearer. It
was only when Alice, thoroughly disgusted, strode off
in the opposite direction that she approached the hill.
And this, more or less, parallels the psychological
experience of modern man.

Melville Harcourt 1909-1984, **Thirteen for Christ**

LIES

> The ancient lie that lust is love
> And passion what it seems.
>> *G. A. Studdert Kennedy 1883–1929, The Unutterable Beauty*

> The cruellest lies are often told in silence.
>> *Robert Louis Stevenson 1850–1894*

> A lie which is half a truth is ever the blackest of lies.
>> *Alfred, Lord Tennyson 1809–1892*

> There is an idea abroad among moral people that they should make their neighbours good. One person I have to make good: myself. But my duty to my neighbour is much more really expressed by saying that I have to make him happy if I may.
>> *Robert Louis Stevenson 1850–1894*

> The three-quarter truth is the most difficult lie.

> They always speak well of you yet they do not really care about you.
>> *Jeremiah 12:2, Good News Bible*

LIFE

> I took my burden to the Lord
> to cast and leave it there,
> I knelt and told him of my plight
> and wrestled deep in prayer.
> But rising up to go my way
> I felt a deep despair
> For as I tried to trudge along
> my burden was still there.
> Why didn't you take my burden Lord?
> Oh won't you take it please.
> Again I asked the Lord for help
> His answering words were these.
> My child, I want to help you out;

I long to take your load.
I want to bear your burdens too
as you walk along life's road.
But this you must remember,
This one thing you must know;
I cannot take your burden
Until you let it go.

Corrie Ten Boom 1892–1983, 'He's More Than Able'

The most difficult lesson of life is to learn to accept the commonplace.

Anonymous

The art of living
is to remember
what to forget.

I never realised that fame
May prove an empty hollow game —
That wealth, despite all it can do
But rarely brings contentment too —
That beauty, though its power be strong,
Will not hide emptiness for long.
I did not guess that every deed
Writes on the face lines all may read.

I did not know when I was young
A sense of humour is among
Life's greatest gifts; nor did I see
That understanding, sympathy
Of true tried friends will still hold sway
When shallow loves have passed away.
I did not dream pain can lead higher —
That love is stronger than desire.

Author unknown

The more you give — the more you get
The more you laugh — the less you fret
The more you do unselfishly — the more you live
   abundantly

The more of everything you share — the more you'll
   always have to spare
The more you love — the more you'll find
that life is good — and friends are kind
For *only* what we give away
Enriches us from day to day.

Anonymous

Life is like a caterpillar laboriously crawling from one
side of a floor to the other, over what appear to be
endless patches of light and dark — some bigger than
others. Having reached the other side, in due course,
he becomes a butterfly and flies back above the same
floor, only to realise that it is a beautiful Persian carpet!

Anonymous

To yield is to be preserved whole,
To be bent is to become straight,
To be hollow is to be filled,
To be tattered is to be renewed.

Lao Tze b. 604BC

To live life to the end is not a childish task.

Boris Pasternak 1890–1960

In contemplation of created things
by steps we ascend to God.

John Milton 1608–1670

True life is strength that comes through coping with
failure.

Peter Barber-Lomax

It is now clear that science is incapable of ordering life.
A life is ordered by values.

Pandit Nehru 1889–1964

The only enduring realism is other-worldly.

André Malraux 1901–1976

'Prepare the way of the Lord'
Draw near us, heavenly Father, in love and
  understanding . . .

Prepare our hearts to receive you . . .
Let us be still, and know that you are God . . .
Know that you hold us and all our world in your
hands . . .

Be with us, Lord Jesus, when we gather in your
name . . .
Inspire us with your joy and peace . . .
Let all who meet us feel the touch of your grace . . .
  and the power of your love . . .

Come Holy Spirit . . . like a cleansing wind . . .
Blow the remnants of our doubts away . . .
As dead leaves stripped from the trees by autumn
  winds . . .
That they may be ready for new life . . .

Life needs light . . . Christ is our light . . .
and into the warmth of his strengthening power
we bring all those for whom we have
a special concern . . .   Amen.

Marion Esling

What different lots our stars accord
This babe to be hailed and wooed as a lord
And that to be shunned as a leper.

Thomas Hood 1799–1845

That which is most personal and intimate to me is most
universal.   *Anonymous*

Truth cannot be dictated — it can only be discovered.
Beauty cannot be ordered — it can only be revealed.
Goodness cannot be commanded — it can only be given.

Anonymous

Life is not a series of problems; it is a network of
mysteries.   *Gabriel Marcel*

May my life be one link in a chain of goodness.
Sabbath Morning Service,
Forms of Prayer for Jewish Worship

Lord a mystery surrounds my life. What comes before it
and what lies after it are hidden from me.

My life is very short, and your universe is vast. But
in the darkness is your presence, and in the mystery
your love.

In every place, at every time, your voice speaks
within me. It leads me in the way of honesty and
charity. It shows me truth and goodness. There are
times when it is hard to hear you, and times when it is
hard to follow you; and I know this is my loss.

In the quietness of this time I turn my thoughts to
you.

Help me to hear your voice, to find your image in my
soul, and to be at peace. Amen.
Sabbath Morning Service II,
Forms of Prayer for Jewish Worship

Choosing life

I call heaven and earth to witness against you this day,
that I have set before you life and death, blessing and
curse; therefore choose life, that you and your
descendants may live, loving the Lord your God,
obeying his voice, and cleaving to him; for that means
life to you and length of days.
Deuteronomy 30:19-20

LISTENING

Listen for the meaning beneath the words.

How can you expect to keep your powers of hearing
when you never want to listen? That God should have
time for you, you seem to take as much for granted as
that you cannot have time for him.
Dag Hammarskjöld 1905–1961

Give every man thine ear, but few thy voice.
William Shakespeare 1564–1623

LONELINESS

Pray that your loneliness may spur you into finding
something to live for, great enough to die for.

Dag Hammarskjöld 1905–1961

People are lonely because they build walls instead of
bridges.

J. F. Newton

There is none more lonely than the man who loves only
himself.

Abraham Ezra

LONGING

The answer to longing is loving.

Lord I am longing to see all your promises fulfilled and
all your people one.

LOOKING

Lord teach me how important it is to look people in the
eyes, smile, and hold it.   Amen.

LORD'S PRAYER, The

In our actions, we should accord with the will of
heaven.   *Chinese aphorism*

Our Father who art in heaven,
hallowed be thy name.
Thy kingdom come.
Thy will be done
on earth as it is in heaven.
Give us this day our daily bread;
and forgive us our trespasses,
as we forgive those who trespass against us.
And lead us not into temptation:
but deliver us from evil.

For thine is the kingdom,
the power and the glory,
for ever and ever.   Amen.

Our Father of heaven
I wish everybody to respect you.
I hope your instruction will be carried out
   on earth as it is in heaven.
Today you send us our daily food.
You wish to cancel our debts
   just like we cancel the debts of other people.
You save us from dangers.
Everything depends on you.
Father, for ever.   Amen.

Chinese version

Let thy will be done upon the earth,
Let it be the same accord
with that of heaven . . .

Maori version

Paraphrase of the Lord's Prayer

O God far above and beyond our grasp, yet close to us
like a parent: let the time come soon when you are
recognised by all as God. That is, when you establish
your supreme and good and just rule over your whole
creation.

Yes, let the time come soon when your gracious plan
for salvation becomes a reality on earth, as it now is in
heaven.

While we wait for that day, let us already now enjoy
the foretaste of the messianic banquet as we share in
the bread that sustains our bodies.

In order to make us worthy of that community,
forgive us what we have done wrong to our brothers
and sisters as we have already forgiven those who did
wrong to us; for we know that we are and must be the
mutually forgiven community, your community of these
end times.

And see to it that we are not tested beyond our strength, for we know that satan can destroy us — unless you rescue us out of his ferocious grip.

Rev Krister Stendhal, Professor of Divinity at Harvard University

LOSS

For all sad words of tongue or pen,
The saddest are these: 'It might have been!'

John Greenleaf Whittier 1807–1892 'Maud Muller'

One who cannot lose his heart, will never really find it.

F. L. Lucas 1894–1967

See also Death

Of self respect

Without self-respect there is no real love.

Help me, Lord, to honour and strengthen, day by day, a step at a time, the wonderful potential that is in every being, and no less in me, through him who sustained, encouraged, strengthened and healed, even Jesus Christ our Lord.   Amen.

LOUDNESS

The biggest guns
The strongest lungs
The loudest sirens
The most voices
The hardest muscles
The greatest powers
are false measures of truth.

Benjamin Whichcote (adapted)

LOVE

Man cannot live without love. He remains a being incomprehensible in himself; his life is senseless if love is not revealed to him, if he does not encounter love, if he does not experience it and make it his own, if he does not participate intimately in it. That is why Christ the redeemer 'fully reveals man to himself' . . . so that . . . man finds again the greatness, the dignity and value that belongs to his humanity.

Pope John Paul II

It is ordinary to love the marvellous;
it is marvellous to love the ordinary:

Love's power is that it lets you exist
outside your own body.

Donald Windham, Two People

When you are with a friend whom you love and respect, you try to be your best self.

Dean Inge 1860–1954

That calm so propitious for work and for discipline of the mind seems to me one of the richest results of love.

Marguerite Yourcenar, Memoirs of Hadrian

To love and to be loved the wise would give
All that for which alone the unwise live.

Walter Savage Landor 1775–1864

Only the person who loves his brother dwells in light; there is nothing to make him stumble. But one who hates his brother is in darkness; he walks in the dark and has no idea where he is going, because the darkness has made him blind.

1 John 11:10-11

To love is to meet oneself, and to meet oneself one must be willing to leave oneself and go towards another.

Michel Quoist

Love is the net of truth.

Abu Said

Anyone can love his friends; anyone can love people who are kind to him; the test is 'Love your enemies'.

Archbishop William Temple 1881–1944

By the help of God love grows and deepens with the years.

The Methodist Service Book

Love is most nearly itself
When here and now cease to matter.

T. S. Eliot 1888–1965, 'East Coker'

It is a great gift to bring out love, even greater than loving.

Ann Todd to Ingrid Bergman when she was dying

Love is the secret of life
Jesus is the secret of love.
Love is like a cake. It needs to be cut into to be shared.

'Do you know why everybody loves Celeste [aged 7]?'
'Why?'
'Because she has no strangers in her life.'

Margaret Gilbert

Returned

Lord, thank you for
her slow turning towards me,
her head resting on my shoulder,
her arm once more around me,
her warmth and reassuring presence,
her gentleness and peace and
love returned, and
love.

Never again will you leave me, for my love is your love, my place is your place and my territory yours. Where the sea wind catches your wings, there will mine fly. Where your talons take up prey, there will mine dive. Where the cliffs rise and the sea threatens, there will our wings go together, stronger for being two eagles flying as one. And where our love is, there will our young be, and your need will be mine and mine yours, and our youngs' needs will be forever ours.

William Horwood, The Stonor Eagles

Love's response

Who may sing the song of love?
Those only who give all,
without reserve, hold nothing back,
'tis they who know the joy,
the quickening pain of love;
'tis they who taught by adoration
hold the heart of love,
and touch all loveless hearts to life
by giving love.

Gilbert Shaw 1883–1967

LUST

To be carnally minded is death; but to be spiritually minded is life and peace.

Romans 8:6, Authorised Version

MADNESS

Great wits are sure to madness near allied
And thin partitions do their bounds divide.

John Dryden 1631–1700, 'Absalom and Achitophel'

His madness was not of the head, but heart.

George Gordon Noel, Lord Byron 1788–1824, 'Lara'

Every man is within a hair's-breadth of being mad. For if a man walk with his forefinger out people think him sane, not so if it be his middle finger.

Diogenes 412–323BC

MANKIND

The civilised man is distinguished from the savage
mainly by prudence, or, to use a slightly wider term,
forethought. He is willing to endure present pains for
the sake of future pleasures, even if the future pleasures
are rather distant.   *Bertrand Russell 1872–1970*

The perfect man is spirit-like.   *Nieh Ch'ueh*

The wise man lives a life free from worry.
He does not indulge in anxious doubts.
His light is without display.
His spirit is guileless and pure.

Chuang Tzu 369BC

MAN–WOMAN

Are not male and female, coal and flame? If the coal
does not seek to know the flame, can either fulfil its
destiny?

Chinese aphorism

MANAGING

Lord, I am responsible for managing the work skills of
others and organising my own life. Let me start
properly and caringly by being close to your will and
your way. Give me the same sensitivity and patience,
the same understanding and sincerity, the same
honesty and humour that your son gave to the apostles.
This I ask each day in his name.   Amen.

Lord give me strength to endure,
not speed to run;
give me calmness of spirit
not discontent in tasks;
give me the strength of your holy grace
not insufficiency of self.
Lord give me your love
your will and
your way.

MANNERS

The greater man, the greater courtesy.

Alfred, Lord Tennyson 1809–1892

MARCHES, Protest

Lord, when I believe strongly, I want to show your way is best.

Help me in giving my support and showing my concern for the truth, not to be dogmatic, angry or overbearing, but sincere, generous, and open minded. As my feet go forward in a certain path, let my way be your way through Jesus Christ our Lord.   Amen.

Let truth be in our minds, joy in our hearts, helpfulness in our hands, and reconciliation and peace in our cause.   Amen.

MARRIAGE

It is strange to be us
when I'm hardly me.
Lord give me strength
to let me be
within his love.
I've so much to learn
about me and us
and the way we should turn.
Without his shape
I'm no shape at all;
I'm part of his one
he's part of my all.
You've entrusted me Lord
with a very great soul
that I feel the pull
of the magnificat call.
I ache inside with love of great kind
yet there's a gentle growth
of peace I find . . .
It's good to be us
when I'm nearly me.   *Anonymous*

MARRIAGE, Sacrament of

Marriage is given that husband and wife may comfort and help each other, living faithfully together in need and in plenty, in sorrow and in joy. It is given that with delight and tenderness they may know each other in love, and, through the joy of their bodily union, may strengthen the union of their hearts and lives.

In marriage husband and wife belong to one another, and they begin a new life together in the community. It is a way of life that all should honour, and it must not be undertaken carelessly, lightly or selfishly, but reverently, responsibly and after serious thought.

This is a way of life, created and hallowed by God.

The Marriage Service, Alternative Service Book 1980

Almighty God, giver of life and love, grant us wisdom and devotion in our life together, that we may be to each other a strength in need, a comfort in sorrow, and companion in joy. So unite our wills with your will, and our spirits with your spirit, that we grow together in love and peace all the days of our lives; through Jesus Christ our Lord. Amen.

The Marriage Service, Alternative Service Book 1980 (adapted)

All that I am I give to you,
and all that I have I share with you.

The Marriage Service, Alternative Service Book 1980

Lord, at the quietness of this time, and in the holiness of this place, give your blessing to your children. You have given them youth with its hopes and love with its dreams. May these come true through their faith in each other, and their trust in you. Let them be devoted to each other, and as the years go by, teach them how

great is the joy that comes from sharing, and how deep
the love that grows with giving. May your presence
dwell among them in the warmth of their love, in the
kindness of their home, and in their charity for others.

The Jewish marriage service

All your strength is in your union;
All your danger is in discord;
Therefore be at peace henceforward.

Henry Wadsworth Longfellow 1807–1882

Live together in harmony, live together in love, as
though you had only one mind and one spirit between
you. Never act from motives of rivalry or personal
vanity, but in humility; think more of one another than
you do of yourself.

Philippians 2:2-3

Let there be spaces in your togetherness
And let the winds of the heavens dance between you.
Love one another, but make not a bond of love:
Let it rather be a moving sea between the shores of
    your souls.
Sing and dance together and be joyous, but let each
    one of you be alone,
Even as the strings of a lute are alone though they
    quiver with the same music.

Give your hearts, but not into each other's keeping.
For only the hand of life can contain your hearts.
And stand together yet not too near together:
For the pillars of the temple stand apart,
And the oak tree and the cypress grow not in each
    other's shadow.

Kahlil Gibran 1883–1931, The Prophet

A good marriage must be created. In the marriage, the little things are the big things . . .

It is never being too old to hold hands.
It is remembering to say 'I love you' at least once each day.
It is never going to sleep angry.
It is having a mutual sense of values and common objectives.
It is standing together and facing the world.
It is forming a circle of love that gathers in the whole family.
It is speaking words of appreciation and demonstrating gratitude in thoughtful ways.
It is having the capacity to forgive and forget.
It is giving each other an atmosphere in which each can grow.
It is not only marrying the right person,
It is being the right partner.

Anonymous

MATURITY

The childhood shows the man
As morning shows the day.

John Milton 1608–1674

The truly human man is moral, and the truly human man is a man of prayer. These two activities define man as a human being, and set him apart from the rest of creation.

Richard Holloway

Men must learn to bear a certain portion of uncertainty.

Sigmund Freud 1856–1939

The sign of health for the middle-aged person is not being young; the sign of health is that he prefers his own age — he has no desire to go back.

Anonymous

An ancient family had for its motto just three
words: *think and thank.*

Anonymous

MEALS

Daily

Father, give us this day our daily bread.

Jesus Christ

Teach me each day and each meal to be thankful for
what I receive, and to take nothing for granted.

See also Hospital

On wheels

Father in your great gifts of earthly food and heavenly
manna, be a strength and support, a guide and
assurance to those who provide and those who receive
meals-on-wheels, through him who provided for all in
need, even Jesus Christ our Lord.   Amen.

MEDITATION

Words are the shell, meditation the kernel.
Words are the body of prayer, and meditation its spirit.

Bachya Ibn Pakuda c. 1050-1120

MEMORIES

Bad memories are lessons
Good memories are examples.

Thank you, Lord, for the gift of memory that obliterates
pain, in all its immediate power, ameliorates the
present, and gives promise for the future. Thank you,
Lord.   Amen.

MENTAL ILLNESS

Adults

Lord, the wonder of mind in harmony with body is
truly amazing. But the tyranny that mind can hold over
body is terrible. Help all those in the darkness of
mental instability to be sustained by your power and
ability to change lack of reason into the fulness of love.
In the name of him who showed unceasing love, even
Jesus Christ our Lord.   Amen.

Children

Dear Lord, torture of the mind and mental anguish are
dark holes in the pattern of creation. But darker still is
the suffering of mental illness in children.

Be a light to their darkness and strength for their
sickness, that your loving heart may be felt and known
in them through all who help them in their disability,
through your infinitely caring son Jesus Christ our
Lord.   Amen.

Let the little children come to me, and do not prevent
them; for of such is the kingdom of heaven. Let the
children come to me.   *Matthew 19:14*

MERRY, The

For the good are always merry,
Save by an evil chance,
And the merry love the fiddle
And the merry love to dance.

W. B. Yeats 1865–1939

MIRACLES

As the floating drop of water is subjected to the effect
of cold, there appears the delicate form of the water
crystal as a three-pointed or six-pointed star. The form
is present before the shape appears.   *Carus*

You find it difficult to believe in miracles? I, on the
contrary, find it easy. They are to be expected. The

starry worlds in time and space, the pageant of life, the processes of growth and reproduction, the instincts of animals, the inventiveness of nature, the rising and the setting sun, the affections and passions, the character of thought, of will, of intuition, consciousness, these singly and together plunge the human mind into profound amazement. Miracles piled upon miracles.

Expound to me, how, for example, a stimulus to a nerve produces a sensation, by what process we recall a name or a fact, 'how a peacock's tail builds up a series of perfect eyes out of hundreds of separate feathers, each with its thousands of separate branches'.

Miracles? For my part I see miracles everywhere.
W. Macneile Dixon, The Human Situation

I am passionately involved in life. I love its change, its colour, its movement. To be alive, to be able to see, to walk, to have a home, music, paintings — it's all a miracle.

I have adopted the technique of living from miracle to miracle. What people get out of me is an outlook on life which comes out in my music.
Arthur Rubinstein 1887–1982, Way of Life

MISERY

Lord give me strength in this misery to know your patience to endure, your power to trust, your will to overcome, your gift to give peace; through Jesus Christ our Lord.   Amen.

Father am I miserable because
life is mostly me and not mostly *you?*

MISFORTUNE

The three great misfortunes in life are:
in youth, to bury one's father;
at middle age, to lose one's wife;
and being old, to have no sons or daughters.
Chinese aphorism

MOCKERY

The strongest can never be strong enough always to be mocked, unless he transforms strength into right, and obedience into duty.

Melville Harcourt 1909-1984

MONEY

The dangers gather as the treasures rise.

Samuel Johnson 1709–1784

The most grievous kind of destitution is to want money in the midst of wealth.

Seneca 4BC–65AD

Money is like muck, not good unless it be spread.

Sir Francis Bacon 1561–1626

Money speaks sense in a language all nations understand.

Aphra Behn 1640–1689, first English professional woman author

So long as all the invested wealth which modern progress brings goes but to build up great fortunes, to increase luxury and make sharper the contrast between the House of Have and the House of Want, progress is not real and cannot be permanent.

Henry George 1839–1897

His best companions, innocence and health;
And his best riches, ignorance of wealth.

Oliver Goldsmith 1728–1774, 'The Deserted Village'

MORALITY

Greyness only belongs to a climate of cold and fog. The moral world is not grey; it is a region of colour, where the shadows are very black indeed, because the sunshine is very bright.

T. R. Glover

MORNING

> Earth has not anything to show more fair:
> Dull would he be of soul who could pass by
> A sight so touching in its majesty:
> This city now doth like a garment wear
> The beauty of the morning.

> *William Wordsworth 1770–1850,*
> *'Composed upon Westminster Bridge'*

O God, creator of light: at the rising of your sun this morning, let the greatest of all lights, your love, rise like the sun within our hearts.

> *Prayer of the Armenian Apostolic Church*

Today is the first day of the rest of your life.

> *Anonymous*

> Morning has broken
> like the first morning.

> Mine is the sunlight
> Mine is the morning
> Born of the one light.

> Praise with elation
> Praise every morning
> God's re-creation
> Of the new day!   *Eleanor Farjeon 1881–1965*

> New every morning is the love
> Our wakening and uprising prove;
> Through sleep and darkness safely brought
> Restored to life, and power, and thought.

> *John Keble 1792–1866*

Greet the morning with hope and high expectation, even if the weather is dull.

Every morning put your mind into your heart and stand in the presence of God all the day long.

> *Julian of Norwich 1342–1413*

For the duties that await me today, I ask your strength
  and skill.
For the things that puzzle me at this moment, I ask
  your patience.
For tasks that have become tedious, I ask your gift of
  perseverance.

Let me remember all this day:
That people matter more than things;
That monetary reward matters less than honest service;
That faith and hope and love are the lasting things,
And the greatest of these is love.

On waking
Glory be to thee my Lord and my God;
For sleep and rest throughout the past night:
For the recurring miracle of daybreak:
For thy promise to be with us wherever we are:
For thy nearness in every circumstance that will make
  up this working day:
For thy changelessness in love and power and peace.

Traditional

For our work

Help us this day, O Lord, to glorify thee in whatever
  we have to do.
Give us skill for the work of our hands;
Concentration for the work of our minds;
Vision in our planning,
Care in detail,
Serenity in meeting the unexpected,
And imagination in dealing with all whom we meet
  this day. *Traditional*

Dedication

Accept, O Lord, this offering of ourselves, our talents,
our knowledge, our intentions throughout the coming
hours.

  Grant us thy blessing in all our thoughts, words and
deeds, that we may learn something new of thy
wisdom and truth, and come to thee at nightfall with
no regrets. *Traditional*

Grace

Go before us, O Lord, in all our doings with thy most
gracious favour, and further us with thy continual help;
that in all our work begun, continued and ended in
thee, we may evermore glorify thy holy name. Through
Jesus Christ our Lord.   *Traditional*

Heavenly Father, our lover and creator, in whom we
live and move and have our being, at whose touch
darkness gives place to light and night to day, lay thy
morning hand on all our faculties which sleep and fill
them with the light of life.
                    Bishop Charles Henry Brent 1862–1929

With prayers and thanks we turn to you to make this
day holy. Wipe away our sins in your mercy, and
strengthen our work for good. Cleanse us from
selfishness, and give us new longing for all that is good
and true. Enlighten the darkness that lies within us,
and bring a blessing to our homes and to those we love.
    Sabbath Evening Service, Forms of Prayer for Jewish Worship

MOVING (house, flat etc)

Lord, in the joy or bereavement of moving house, give
me the calm reassurance of your presence to guide,
choose well, organise thoughtfully and with
imagination; to keep my humour and resolve high, my
irritability and impatience low, to help others always
and to understand well, that in your plan of creation
chaos came before darkness, and darkness before
light.   Amen.

MUSIC

As a conductor and musicians are part of one orchestra,
as limbs and muscles, sinews and blood part of one
body, help us to see that each of us is important to
creation as a whole; that your rhythms and your tempo

are music to our lives as long as we keep in harmony
with you, now and through all eternity.   Amen.

Music that gentler on the spirit lies
Than tired eyelids upon tired eyes.

Alfred, Lord Tennyson 1809–1872

NARROW-MINDEDNESS

The person who is narrow of vision cannot be big-
hearted.

Chinese aphorism

NASTINESS

One of the worst things about life is not how nasty the
nasty people are. You know that already. It is how
nasty the nice people can be.

Anthony Powell

My God, keep my tongue from causing harm and lips
from telling lies. Let me be silent if people curse me,
my soul still humble and at peace with all.

Daily Amidah (Standing Prayer)
Forms of Prayer for Jewish Worship

Corrective to being nasty

Let the words of my mouth and the meditation of my
  heart be now and always acceptable to you,
Lord, my strength and my redeemer.

Psalm 19:14

Ceasing being nasty

Lord of all true power and real strength, remove from
us every habit and inclination to be nasty, vindictive or
mean. Help us to know that your way is sufficient and
in giving your kindness, your thoughtfulness and your
joy we are providing further threads in the tapestry of
your service and your love.   Amen.

NATURE

Blessed are you, Lord our God, king of the universe,
who creates fragrant plants, different kinds of spices,
sweet smelling oil.

Forms of Prayer for Jewish Worship

Blessed are you, Lord our God, king of the universe,
who makes us holy through doing his commands
and commands us concerning washing our hands;
who creates the fruit of the vine;
who brings forth food out of the earth;
who creates different kinds of food;
who creates the fruit of the tree;
who creates the fruit of the earth;
by whose word all things exist.
Blessed are you the life of all existence.

Forms of Prayer for Jewish Worship

NEIGHBOURHOOD

It is good manners that constitute the excellence of a
neighbourhood.

Confucius (K'ung Fu-tze) 551–479BC

Father, help me in this neighbourhood to search
for those things that make for community. A
shared life is fulfilling. If I do not use my abilities I
will atrophy and then never know the potential
and joy of what you have so generously given, in
the example of Jesus Christ our Lord.   Amen.

NERVOUSNESS

As a carpenter takes a grip of his implements, as a
musician confidently raises his instrument, take me,
Lord, and give me your son's confidence in you, so that
his accord with you sings in my life, now and every
day.   Amen.

This nervousness, Lord, is so silly when I think about it, but my emotions are high, my anticipation great, and so little of me in control.

Perhaps, Lord, that is what you prefer, little of *me* in control, which leaves more space for you to redirect my emotions and channel them into right appreciation and true understanding.

Lord, help me to understand that the power of my emotions should be calmed and directed by your love, and make this my trust and confidence — through Jesus Christ our Lord. Amen.

NEWNESS

Lord help me not to feel threatened by the newness of things. The seasons change, new life must come to replace the old and worn out, and I must grow. Amen.

NIGHT

Night and those endless fallings, Lord, the semi-conscious dreams of running but never being fast enough, or too fast with no one there. Give me faith to conquer the lonely agony of my fears, and lack of trust in you, so that with the coming of day there may be new insight and renewed trust through Jesus Christ. Amen.

How beautiful is night!
A dewy freshness fills the silent air;
No mist obscures, nor cloud, nor speck, nor stain,
Breaks the serenity of heaven.

Robert Southey 1774–1843

Long insights in pensive discontent.

Edmund Spenser 1552–1599

Lord in the Garden of Gethsemane you met darkness and difficulty, solitary wondering and anguish, fearful imaginings and endless moments.

Without the Father you could not have continued. Only by being near to him could you learn from being in the darkness, and summon courage to continue in the strength which he alone supplies. Give me such strength and courage now through your example which is power through all eternity.   Amen.

For children
Through the night your angels kept
Watch beside me while I slept;
Now the dark has passed away;
Thank you, Lord, for this new day.

Priest's Vade Mecum (adapted)

Good night! Good night!
For flies the light;
But still God's love
Shall flame above,
Making all bright.
Good night! Good night!

Anonymous

I will lay me down in peace and take my rest;
For it is thou Lord only, that makest me dwell in safety.

Psalm 4:8

NIGHTMARES
Nuclear
Lord, I do not know how to protest against this nightmare of nuclear proliferation. So perhaps, Lord, your protest will convince where mine is hopeless.

Therefore, Lord, let 300 or 400 or 500 people meet each Sunday for the eucharist at centres where missiles are based, so that your contrasting perspective may be unmistakably seen.

I believe passionately in your peace, your truth, your way, for ever in Jesus Christ our Lord.   Amen.

Just a little rain falling all around
The grass lifts its head to the heavenly sound
Just a little rain
What have they done to the rain?

Just a little boy standing in the rain
The gentle rain that falls for years
And the grass is gone, the boy disappears
And the rain keeps falling like helpless tears.
And what have they done to the rain?

Malrina Reynolds

Personal
Just as I am
O Jesus Christ, I come.
It is dark —
so dark.
I am sinking and filled with heaviness.
My whole being is weighed down.
I am deafened by my heart beat
which tells me life goes on.
Outside these walls it is winter,
cold and grey.
Inside the long dark night of the soul.
I cannot escape, I am a prisoner
all ways are blocked;
and they have taken my pills away.
I am numb and cold and do not move.
I long for the peace of sleep which will blot out my
    misery.
It does not come to comfort me.
I watch the dawn,
the sky flushed with pink fades into the light of day.
Another day.
Gradually, slowly, over the days my head clears,
my body lightens,
my spirit is free.
I notice the spring flowers;
I enjoy a bath;
I appreciate a meal.

The colour has returned to my world.
Just as I am.
O Jesus Christ, I come.

Gillian Packington

NOISE

I cannot move, and the noise gets worse. Lord, this
noise is driving me crazy, endless, insistent, loud,
unremitting. What can I do?

If I run from it, I am overwhelmed. But . . . if I face it,
slide into its rhythms, sing to it, speak to it, pray
through it, for others in similar distress, its power is
curtailed; and you, Lord, are there with me, as you
were long ago at the noise that surrounded the
explosive power of the silent cross.   Amen.

OBEDIENCE

Blessed are you, Lord our God, king of the universe,
who makes us holy through doing his commands.

Forms of Prayer for Jewish Worship

OBSERVATION

When you see a good man, emulate him;
When you see a bad man, examine yourself.

Anonymous

'OFF', Feeling
Everything

Lord I feel 'off' everything.
Either I need nothing,
a doctor or you.
If I need nothing then
show me.
If I need a doctor then
lead me.
If I need you then
correct me

inform me
love me
hold me
now and
always.   Amen.

Food

This may be a sign, Lord, that I ought to eat and drink
more sparingly. Help me, Lord, to do just that, and
thereby appreciate your gifts all the more, through the
example of Jesus Christ our Lord.   Amen.

People

Lord, I may have been just too involved with people,
used them as a substitute or prop, a sounding board or
escape. Help me in this time of reflection to value
silence and being alone, reflection and peace, so that
when I learn from this lesson I may value people more
and you above all, in your blessed son Jesus Christ our
Lord.   Amen.

ONESELF

What can I give him
  poor as I am?
If I were a shepherd
  I would bring a lamb;
If I were a wise man
  I would do my part;
Yet what can I give him —
  give my heart.

Christina Rossetti 1830–1894

OPPORTUNITY

Away with funeral music, set
  The pipe to powerful lips —
The cup of life's for him who drinks
  And not for him who sips.

Anonymous

Die when I may, I want it said of me by those who
knew me best, that I always plucked a thistle and
planted a flower where I thought a flower would grow.

Abraham Lincoln 1809–1865

The waste of life lies in the love we have not given, the
powers we have not used, the selfish prudence that will
risk nothing, and which, shirking pain, misses
happiness as well.

Mary Cholmondeley

Your sea before my sea
Your land before my land
Your time before my time
Your opportunity before my opportunity
Your plan, Lord, to be fulfilled by me.
Let me use this occasion
wisely, lovingly, and well.   Amen.

Anonymous

OUTCASTS

Make me care about the slum-child, the misfit at work,
the people crammed into the mental hospital, the men,
women and youths behind bars. Jar my complacence,
expose my excuses and get me involved in the life of
my community.

Robert Raines

'OFF' DAYS

An 'off' day invariably occurs
because of not having a day off.

A suggested cure

Force yourself to walk slowly down the street, smile
and say, 'Good morning'. Do this to every person you
can. If anyone speaks to you, listen rather than speak,
smile rather than moan, laugh rather than sigh–and see
what happens, *now*.

OFFERING

God has given so much without my asking. This makes me feel poor by comparison and very much second best. Good, that is as it should be.

The answer therefore is not in my inadequacy, which will always be, but in my response — how I receive his gifts and how I give thanks.

Life is your offering, Lord,
beauty, truth, goodness,
love, gentleness, kindness,
are all your offering, Lord.
Now in your example,
let me respond.   Amen.

OVER-ACTIVITY

To realise that the heart of mission is communion with God in the midst of the world's life will save us from the demented activism of these days.

Bishop John Taylor

OVER-CROWDING

You are never so lonely as in the midst of a crowd.

Lord, I am in danger of being squashed and jostled, constricted and desperate. Calm me in the midst of my storm. Let me hear, with great concentration, the quiet assurance of your voice. And lead me out in the power of your hand to an area of abiding peace, in the way of Jesus Christ.   Amen.

OVER-SPENDING

Beware of all enterprises that require new clothes.
Henry David Thoreau 1817–1862

OVERWEIGHT

Unless I am a medical exception, and in this very few

are, help me to understand that if I trusted you more to give me my daily bread, I would eat less, exercise more, worry less and enjoy life more fully, for Christ's sake.   Amen.

Round numbers are always false.
                              Samuel Johnson 1709–1784

PAIN

When pain is to be borne, a little courage helps more than much knowledge, a little human sympathy much more than courage and the least tincture of the love of God more than all.   *C. S. Lewis 1898–1963*

The best is bought at the cost of great pain.
                              Coleen McCullough

Pain makes men think,
thinking gives a man wisdom;
and wisdom confers peace.
                              Boris Pasternak 1890–1960

Pain is as inevitable as accident in a physical world. It is a signal, suited to our animal nature, that something is wrong. It is a warning sign of danger; and if it is to operate efficiently, it must operate consistently.
                              Hugh Montefiore

Another's

Lord I cannot bear this person's pain.
   Like a watcher, stilled and silenced by caring and protecting, I feel as though I were in a garden of long ago where Christ wrestled with agony as disciples drowsily looked on. I feel the helplessness of being a friend powerless, except to pray. I can do nothing: but you Lord can do everything. Be once again, as with your blessed son, the pain-bearer for this person and all humanity.   Amen.

PARDON

Pardon only confers peace when there is complete honesty, true contrition, and a new attitude without demanding anything in return.

O Lord, teach me that the solution to life's problems comes not from the knees but from the heart.

Anonymous

Lord, grant to thy faithful people pardon and peace.

Compline

Her iniquity is pardoned: for she has received from the Lord's hand.

Isaiah 40:2

PARENTS' PRAYER

I have a child to bring up . . .

Help me to perform my task with wisdom and kindness and good cheer. Help me always to see him clearly as he is. Let not my pride in him blind me to his faults. Let not my fear for him magnify my doubts and fears until I make him doubtful and fearful in his turn. Quicken my judgement so that I shall know how to train him to think as a child, to be in all things pure and simple as a child.

I have a child to bring up .. . .

Give me great patience and a long memory. Let me remember the hard places in my own youth, so that I may help when I see him struggling as I struggled then. Let me remember the things that made me glad lest I, sweating in the toil and strain of life, forget that a little child's laughter is the light of life.

I have a child to bring up . . .

Teach me that love that understandeth all things. The love that knows no weakness, tolerates no selfishness.

Keep me from weakening my child by granting him pleasures that end in pain, ease of body that must bring sickness of soul, a vision of life that must end in death. Grant that I love my child wisely and myself not at all.

I have a child to bring up . . .

Give him the values and beauty and just reward of industry. Give him an understanding brain and hands that are cunning to work out his happiness.

I have a child to bring up . . .

Help me to send him into the world with a mission of service. Strengthen my mind and heart that I may teach him that he is his brother's keeper. Grant that he may serve those who know not the need of service, and, not knowing, need it the more.

I have a child to bring up . . .

So guide and direct me that I may do this to the glory of God, and to my child's happiness.

Assembly Workshop, *9:11*

PARENTS

Aging

Lord, my mother is irritating at the same age that her mother was also.

My father repeats himself endlessly in every way.

Lord, what makes me so attractive is that I'm imitating both already. Amen.

Lord, there is not much of my father that has not been replaced by medical science, but that makes the essential him all the more precious, and that essential him is you, Lord. Thank you.

Of an aging mother

Eyesight is failing,
Kitchen's the same;
Hair is thinning,
Cleaning's the same.

Hearing is faulty,
TV's the same;
Chewing's painful,
Weather's the same;
Memory is fading,
Yet I'm the same:
Thank you Lord.   Amen.

Mothers

Lord, we thank you for our mothers
and the gift of
their tenderness and understanding
their patience and thoughtfulness
their kindness and love.

We can be so wilful
so thoughtless
so impatient
and so unkind.
For often we demand without grace
and receive without thanks
and always we expect more.
We expect our mother to be there
to cater to our selfishness,
and then we wonder
why she gets tired
and irritable
and thoroughly fed up.
Yet through all these things she loves us.

Lord, teach us to be thoughtful and understanding
and sensitive to our mother's needs,
that we may ease her days

and increase her joy.
We ask this through the generous and loving
example of our saviour Jesus Christ.   Amen.

PATIENCE

We need patience to listen properly to others.
We need patience to love,
We need patience to attend properly
   to writers, to painters, who tell
   us about the times in which we live.
We need patience to listen to God.
God, give us patience.

Monica Furlong

God's ways seem dark, but soon or late
They touch the shining hills of day;
The evil cannot brook delay
The good can well afford to wait.

John Greenleaf Whittier 1807–1892

Lord, teach me to be patient, no matter how long and
hard the situation may be.

Love is patient, love is kind.   *1 Corinthians 13:4*

For patience, meditate on a watch.

Great hearts should be patient under misfortune as well
as joyful when all goes well.

Miguel de Cervantes 1547–1616,
Sancho Panza in Don Quixote

PEACE

Three conditions for the peace of God:
1 Anxiety for nothing.
2 Prayerfulness for everything.
3 Thanksgiving for anything.

Anonymous

Help us to clear a space and to listen to the things that calm us.

In God's eyes the man stands high who makes peace between men.   *Talmud*

Loving Spirit, give me serenity and a quiet heart. In times of stress and anxiety give me your tranquillity, and even in disaster hold me in your loving strength which alone can give true peace.   Amen.

Be utterly humble and you shall hold the foundation of peace.   *Chinese aphorism*

A sound man not advancing himself endlessly becomes himself.   *Chinese aphorism*

The Lord's my shepherd, I'll not want;
He makes me down to lie
In pastures green; he leadeth me
The quiet waters by.

My soul he doth restore again,
And me to walk doth make
Within the paths of righteousness,
E'en for his own name's sake.

Yea, though I walk in death's dark vale,
Yet will I fear no ill;
For thou are with me, and thy rod
And staff me comfort still.

My table thou hast furnished
In presence of my foes;
My head thou dost with oil anoint,
And my cup overflows.

Goodness and mercy all my life
Shall surely follow me,
And in God's house for evermore
My dwelling-place shall be.

                              Psalm 23, Scottish Psalter 1650

or

1 The Lord is my shepherd; therefore can I lack
   nothing.
2 He shall feed me in a green pasture, and lead me
   forth beside the waters of comfort.
3 He shall convert my soul, and bring me forth in the
   paths of righteousness for his name's sake.
4 Yea, though I walk through the valley of the shadow
   of death, I will fear no evil; for thou art with me, thy
   rod and thy staff comfort me.
5 Thou shalt prepare a table before me against them
   that trouble me; thou hast anointed my head with
   oil, and my cup shall be full.
6 But thy loving kindness and mercy shall follow me all
   the days of my life; and I will dwell in the house of
   the Lord for ever.

(Glory be to the Father, and to the Son and to the Holy
Spirit. As it was in the beginning is now and ever shall
be world without end.   Amen)

Book of Common Prayer

Challenge us, Lord,
across the frontiers of the world
through the voices of strangers
through the things we do not always like to hear or do
through the lives of people of other faiths and cultures,
in the simplicity of children
the questioning of young people
the wisdom of the old.
Make us your pilgrim people, Lord
and give us courage to take the leaps of faith
you ask of us today.   *Anonymous*

Lord Jesus, we thank you that you left your Father's
glory and became poor that we through your poverty
might become rich.
   We pray for all those who are away from home in
your name.
   Grant them to know the peace of your presence, the

blessedness of poverty, the glory of obedience, for your
sake and the sake of all the world.   *Anonymous*

Lord, we pray for peace,
not peace at any price,
but peace at your price.
Make us and all your children
so rich with your love
your generosity
your justice
that we can afford
to pay the cost of peace.   *Anonymous*

Dear Father in heaven
let us be peacemakers
more ready to call people friends than enemies
more ready to trust than to mistrust
more ready to love than to hate
more ready to respect than to despise
more ready to serve than to be served
more ready to absorb evil than to pass it on.
Dear Father in heaven
let us be more like Christ.   Amen.   *Anonymous*

Jesus does not give us all the answers, but he takes
away the questions and gives us peace.

Henry Burgin

This, I say, is the stillness:
A retreat to one's roots;
Or better yet, return
To the will of God.

Tao Te Ching No. 16, tr. R. B. Blakney

Deep peace of the running wave to you.
Deep peace of the flowing air to you.
Deep peace of the quiet earth to you.
Deep peace of the shining stars to you.
Deep peace of the Son of Peace to you.

Anonymous

Endeavour to keep the unity of the Spirit in the bond of peace.

Ephesians 4:3

Christ is our peace.
He has reconciled us to God
in one body by the cross.
We meet in his name
and share his peace.

Rite A, Alternative Service Book 1980

Look to water. What is more yielding? Yet it comes back again to wear down the most rigid stone. What is more forceful than quiet water?

Chinese, traditional

In the home

Peace to this house and to all who dwell in it.

Traditional

Peace and quiet

Amid the roar of traffic and the rushing of the crowd, comes stillness and peace and quiet when we are centred on you, Lord.   Amen.

See also Isaiah 17:12. See also Quiet.

PEOPLE

A person is an irreplaceable centre of caring.

PERCEPTION

Though a man may be utterly stupid, he is very perspicacious when reprehending the bad actions of others; though he may be very intelligent, he is dull enough while excusing his own faults.

Chinese aphorism

PERFECTION

To blame what is honest and just is called seriously
harming oneself. To pretend not to be able to be
constantly perfect nor to observe justice, is to let oneself
go.

Perfection is the quiet house, justice the straight way
of man.

To leave empty and not live in the peaceful house, to
abandon and not follow the narrow way is deplorable!

The way of virtue is near us; it is the natural law
which is engraved in our hearts; some go far to seek it.
It is easy to practise virtue; some make it difficult.

Mencius (Meng-K'o) 372–289BC

PERSEVERANCE

Perseverance gains the prize.   *Chinese aphorism*

Let us remain aware of our task and not grumble, a
solution will come. Now I know that first and foremost
I shall require courage and cheerfulness.

Anne Frank 1929–1945

Give us grace and strength to forbear and to persevere.
Give us courage and gaiety and the quiet mind,
spare us to our friends, soften us to our enemies.

Robert Louis Stevenson 1850–1894

In comradeship

Clear before us through the darkness
  Gleams and burns the guiding light;
Brother clasps the hand of brother,
  Stepping fearless through the night.

B. S. Ingemann 1789–1862, tr. S. Baring-Gould 1834–1924

Blessed Lord, who for my sake was content to bear
sorrow and want and death, grant me such a measure
of your spirit that I may follow you in all self-denial
and tenderness of soul.   Amen.

Bishop Brooke Foss Westcott 1825–1901 (adapted)

O God of all goodness and grace, worthy of a greater
love than I can either give or understand, fill my heart
with such love for you, that nothing may seem too hard
for me to do or to suffer in obedience to you.

Grant that I may become daily more like you, and
finally obtain that serenity of life which you have
promised to those who love you; through Jesus Christ
our Lord.   Amen.

Bishop Brooke Foss Westcott 1825-1901 (adapted)

PERSPECTIVE

Cease denying, begin knowing,
Comes peace this way . . .

Cecil Day-Lewis 1904–1972

We are living under the still impenetrable cloud of the
holocaust and in the century of the refugee.

*Rabbi Hugo Gryn, Preface to
Forms of Prayer for Jewish Worship*

Join this piety of the world which died in the holocaust
to the spirit which has arisen from its ashes.

*Rabbis Lionel Blue and Jonathan Magonet
editors, Forms of Prayer for Jewish Worship*

Consider what a man is within, not without, see him as
a creature of God.   *Roger Bush*

O Father we welcome your words,
And we will take heart for the future,
Remembering the past.   *T. S. Eliot 1888–1965*
                    Chorus VIII, Choruses from 'The Rock'

Man is joined spirit and body,
And therefore must serve as spirit and body.

T. S. Eliot 1888–1965
Chorus IX, Choruses from 'The Rock'

All our knowledge brings us nearer to our ignorance,
All our ignorance brings us nearer to death,

But nearness to death no nearer to God.
Where is the life we have lost in living.

> *T. S. Eliot 1888–1965*
> Chorus I, *Choruses from 'The Rock'*

Do not condemn us to be alone when together.
Allow us to be together when alone.

Archbishop Helder Camara, A Thousand Reasons for Living

In every heart there is a cross and a throne and each is occupied. If Jesus is on the throne, ruling, self is on the cross dying.

But if self is being obeyed, and so is ruling, then it is on the throne. And the self on the throne means that Jesus has been put on the cross.   *S. D. Gordon*

Even behind the darkest cloud there is sunlight — until evening, when even behind the darkest night there is the promise of another dawn.

God of all strength and harmony, teach me to find the deep springs of laughter in generosity and understanding. Give to me the grace and courage of laughter that seeks to heal and not to hurt; that sees the unimportance of trifles instead of magnifying them; that gives me a sense of proportion by helping me to see not myself but you at the centre of all things. I ask this in the name of your son who is the lord of joy, Jesus Christ our Lord.   Amen.

Do not give me riches, God, that may make me proud; nor poverty that may deject me.

Give me, God, some help that I may serve you, and life that I may praise you and death that I may find salvation.   *Marrano*

Your unlovingness is not contributing to my wholeness.

All are but parts of one stupendous whole.

> *Alexander Pope 1688–1744, 'An Essay on Man'*

In the last lingering years I shall need very few
things. A single rug to warm me through the
winter; one meal to last me the whole day. It does
not matter that my house is rather small; you
cannot sleep in more than one room. It does not
matter that I have not many horses; one cannot
ride on two horses at once. As contented a one
among a hundred men, look as you may, you will
not find one.   *Po-Chu-i 835AD*

Yesterday is affirmation
Today is opportunity
Tomorrow is hope.

POLLUTION

To harm the earth is to heap contempt on its creator.
  Man did not weave the web of life, he is merely a
strand of it. Whatever he does to the web, he does to
himself.
  Henceforth give the rivers the kindness you would
give your brother.

                              Chief Seattle 1854

POSSIBILITY

It is not the ability we have that is important, but the
availability.

POVERTY

Lord, I have only recently discovered that many in
other places are poor because I am comfortable, and my
society and its systems perpetuate the problem.
  Though I can do little, help me to behave
honourably, spend reasonably and give generously to
those agencies which truly ensure relief and care,
regular support and encouragement to those in need,
through Jesus Christ our Lord.   Amen.

Lord help me to offer first respect and then
aid.   Amen.

True poverty is lack of love, lack of opportunity, lack of
peace.

The poor of the world are my body, he said,
To the end of the world they shall be
The bread and the blankets you give to the poor
You'll find you have given to me, he said,
  You'll find you have given to me.

Sydney Carter, 'Judas and Mary'

Have you seen the old man
Who walks the streets of London
Kicking up papers in his worn-out shoes
In his eyes you see no pride
His hands hung loosely by his side
Yesterday's papers, telling yesterday's news
So how can you tell me you're lonely
And say for you that the sun don't shine
So let me take you by the hand
And lead you through the streets of London
And I'll show you something
That should help you change your mind.

Ralph McTell

When you give to the poor, it is like lending to the
Lord, and the Lord will pay you back.

Proverbs 19:17

POWER

Be careful of those in power! For they draw no man
near them except in their own interest.
   They seem like friends when it is to their advantage,
but they do not stand by a man in his hour of need.

Sayings of the Fathers, Forms of Prayer for Jewish Worship

PRAYER

How to pray

Slow down
Be still
Wait attentively
Listen lovingly
Ask
Seek
Knock
Be opened
Stay prayer-filled
    and alert.

Lord teach me to forget all but you when I pray.

A man must purify his heart before he prays.

Exodus Rabbah

Difficulty in prayer

Do not worry about having few words or nothing to say. The fewer the words the more chance of listening for God to speak.

As craftsmen take time sharpening their implements before and after their work and preparing carefully for the next day, so we ought to prepare to listen before praying.   Amen.

When you cannot pray with the proper concentration, try your utmost to speak the words in a spirit of belief in their truth.

Nachman of Bratzlav 1772–1811

Prayer and life

When I was at school, we used to practise setting dry grass on fire with a magnifying glass. If I remember correctly, you had to learn to hold the glass at exactly the right angle to the sun and the right distance from the ground. It wasn't all that difficult, but it took practice and persistence.

In this simple way, the heat of the sun was focused sufficiently to produce a specific result. No focusing, no fire. This experience has remained with me as an image of prayer, more particularly the relationship between prayer and action.

Christians are the magnifying glasses of the love of God, means by which that love can be focused on particular people and needs; prayer is the way we bring that love and that need into precise focus, so that God's will can better be done.

Bishop Ronald Bowlby

Prayer clothes a man in the garment of holiness, evokes the light and fire implanted within him by his maker, illumines his whole being and unifies the lower and higher worlds.

Zohar, 13th century (adapted)

Man without God is a seed upon the wind.

T. S. Eliot 1888–1965

Prayer is the key that unlocks heaven and opens the door to a deep understanding of human life.

Bishop Charles Henry Brent 1862–1929

Is prayer your steering wheel or your spare tyre?

Corrie Ten Boom 1892–1983

Prayer is to the soul what food is to the body.

True prayer is exposure to the purposes of God.

Prayer is something you do; it is a style of living.

Bishop John Taylor

Action should be something added to the life of prayer, not something taken away from it.

Thomas Aquinas 1225–1274

I am praying (to the tune of 'Sailing')

I am praying,
I am saying,
home is you, Lord,
every day.
I am praying,
I am staying,
always near you
to be free.

I am here, Lord,
you are near, Lord,
in the bread and
in the wine.
You have blessed me,
and caressed me,
filled my life with
life divine.

Send me out, Lord,
in the power
of your Spirit
to do your will.
Let your joy be
forever in me
and such giving
be my fill.

We will love you
Lord for ever;
let us ever
sing your praise.

In the knowledge
that we love you
and you'll love us
all our days.

We cannot hate those for whom we have learnt to pray.

To travel prayerfully is to arrive thankfully.

Anonymous

He prayeth best who leaves unguessed
The mystery of another's breast.
Why cheeks grow pale, why eyes o'er flow,
Or heads are white, thou needs't not know.
Enough to know by many a sign
That every heart hath needs like thine.

John Greenleaf Whittier 1807–1892

PRESSURE

Lord, when under pressure give me your calm, your
peace, your resilience, your quickened awareness and
sustain my trust in you, now and always.   Amen.

PRIDE

Pride, the never-failing vice of fools.

Alexander Pope 1688–1744

PRIESTS (or others in a pastoral role)

Since a priest comes in the name of God who is love he
should try to be loving, cheerful and warm, without
being overbearing or timid or rude. He is not there to
be popular or to grovel or be anything other than
Christ's willing servant. He represents Jesus and the
Church. In every situation, however serious or casual,
he should feel that he is walking, talking and being
sustained with God's power and that as God's peace
begins and continues, so it ends the time spent. He and
God have entered into a continual partnership. If in
doubt he should be calm, listen, and observe.

He belongs to the only profession that is called upon
to give time. He must therefore never be in a hurry or
be anxious. He must always be prepared to listen
carefully, accurately, lovingly and often, touching each
occasion with the spirit of Christ.

Because Christ has won all the victories needful to
salvation the priest of Christ can relax while being
vigilant even in the face of apparently insoluble

problems. He can dare to be happy and not be afraid of apparently doing nothing. As a good shepherd he must take time, in fulfilment of his ordination vow, to think, read and reflect, to visit, especially when it is not an emergency, looking at all times to Christ to guide and complete every aspect.

He must give prayerful parts of each day to God, lovingly, cheerfully, thankfully, especially at the beginning, in the middle and at the end.

He should not be afraid to offer and lead people to the sacraments or to hand over what is left undone of his work, his day, and his life to God and pray thankfully for all.

To live in the midst of the world
    without desiring its pleasures;
To be a member of each family
    yet belonging to (n)one;
To share all sufferings;
To penetrate all secrets;
To heal all wounds;
To go from men to God
    and offer him their prayers;
To return from God to men
    to bring them pardon, peace and hope;
To have a heart of fire for charity
    and a heart of bronze for chastity;
To teach and to pardon;
To console and to bless always;
This life of yours;
O priest of Jesus Christ!
                    Henri Dominique Lacordaire 1802–1861

The priest should preach
as a dying man to dying men.
                    Richard Baxter 1615–1691

Come to him, to that living stone, rejected by men but in God's sight chosen and precious; and like living stones be yourselves built into a spiritual house, to be a holy priesthood, to offer spiritual sacrifices acceptable to God through Jesus Christ.

1 Peter 2:4-5

PRISON

Show me the prison
Show me the gaol
Show me the prisoner
Whose life has gone stale
And I'll show you a young man
With so many reasons why
There but for fortune
Go you or I
You or I.

Phil Ochs

Father, prisons are the final admission of walls within ourselves, of actions that have not been thought through and the conscience that has not been trained. Let true justice and fair conditions minister to all who are in prison; correct what can be changed; enlighten what is darkness; and release those justly imprisoned from the wounds of their thoughts and actions, and those unjustly imprisoned from their bitterness and resentment, so that a right spirit may renew what has caused wrong and hurt.   Amen.

PROMISES

Help me to remember, Lord, how much happiness is spread through a promise *kept*.

PROTECTION

Those whom heaven would save, it fences around with gentleness.

Lao Tze 604BC

PURITY

Almighty God,
to whom all hearts are open,
all desires known,
and from whom no secrets are hidden,
cleanse the thoughts of our hearts
by the inspiration of your Holy Spirit,
that we may perfectly love you,
and worthily magnify your holy name;
through Jesus Christ our Lord.   Amen.

Collect for Purity, Alternative Service Book 1980

PURPOSE

Straight on towards heaven to press with single bent,
To know and love my God, and then to die content.
John Henry Newman 1801–1890

What I am is God's gift to me.
What I become is my gift to God.

Anonymous

QUARRELLING

Quarrelling leads to bitterness
Bitterness to resentment
Resentment to anger
Anger to revenge
Revenge to violence
Violence to murder
Murder to death
Death to nothing.
So—don't quarrel.
And if you do—make amends.

QUESTIONING

An unexamined life is not worth living.
Socrates 469–399BC

Do not make a quest for facts a substitute for faith.

There is no deep faith without deep doubting and deep
questioning.

QUIET

In these few moments of quietness, quicken, O God,
my awareness
of your presence;
of your greatness;
of your goodness.
There are lots of things in this life that I love very
much;
There are lots of things that I don't understand;
There are lots of things in which I fall short of my best.
I need your forgiveness;
I need your help now;
I need your love to the end.   Amen.

Rita Snowden (abridged)

Study to be quiet.

1 Thessalonians 4:11

Give me my scallop shell of quiet,
My staff of faith to walk upon.

Sir Walter Raleigh 1552–1618

There's nothing so becomes a man
As modest stillness and humility.

William Shakespeare 1564–1616, Henry V

Drop thy still dews of quietness
Till all our strivings cease;
Take from our souls the strain and stress,
And let our ordered lives confess
The beauty of thy peace.

Breathe through the heats of our desire
Thy coolness and thy balm;

Let sense be dumb, let flesh retire;
Speak through the earthquake, wind and fire,
O still small voice of calm.

John Greenleaf Whittier 1807–1892

Quiet moments

Use the quiet moment when going to work, or
returning home, in worship, hospital, with family and
friends.

RACIAL INTOLERANCE

You can play a tune of sorts on the white piano keys.
You can also play some kind of tune on the black notes.
But for real music, rich in harmony, you must use both
the white and the black notes.

Dr Kodwo Aggrey (Ghana)

Lord thank you for variety in nature, in land and sea.
Thank you for varieties of gifts and limitations within
me and within others. Thank you that others can do
what I cannot and perceive values which I have yet to
learn.

Help me to learn from others, sincerely, attentively,
lovingly and never to scorn what they have to offer. For
everyone has something of value to share. Help me to
find it.   Amen.

Dialogue must probe beyond the glad discovery of
similarities to the more painful recognition of
differences. The deeper the appreciation of this other
faith the greater the knowledge of what these
disagreements really are.

Bishop John Taylor

First, I would say, pay attention to the real conviction
that underlies the precise point at which disagreement
appears and then try to turn mere confrontation of

opposites into a real and possible choice.

Secondly, I must be patient enough to listen and learn until I begin to see the world through the other man's eyes. I must persevere in listening openness.

When I come to appreciate his understanding, I shall be given access to the light and dark places of that stranger's world. And then, at last, I shall see the saviour and Lord of *that* world, my Lord Jesus, and yet not as I have known him. I shall understand how perfectly he matches all needs — he who is the unique Lord and saviour of all possible worlds.

Bishop John Taylor

RAIN

Thank you, Lord, for the cleansing gift of rain, that cuts thirst, saves life, increases growth, cleanses and soothes in quiet waters and renews the earth. Thank you, Lord, for the cleansing gift of rain.   Amen.

And the Holy Spirit

I saw the darkness on the deep
I heard the soft wind blowing
and then I felt the strange stirring
of the Spirit on the waters.

And the rain fell softly and the wind blew gently,
and the wind and the rain were the coming of the
    Spirit.

I saw the bruised man crying,
he said 'The Spirit is on me';
but still they would not listen
and they nailed him in the wind.

And the rain fell softly and the wind blew gently,
and the wind and the rain were the coming of the
    Spirit.

I see the Christ men frightened
for the waters numb are rising;
so hard they search for the Spirit

but they will not feel the wind.
If they only stopped their running,
if they only crawled from out of their shells,
if they only listened to the wind,
and felt the warmth of the gentle rain,
they'd know, yes, they'd know that the wind and the
  rain
that softly surround them
are the Spirit of the caring God
who wants to be always with them.

And the rain fell softly and the wind blew gently,
and the wind and the rain were the coming of the
  Spirit.

Author unknown

RAGE

A man is as big as the things that make him angry.
Winston Churchill 1874–1964

RAPE

Oh God, I feel terrible . . . I feel sick . . . I want to die
. . . I've been raped! Raped! *Raped!* Do you *hear*? . . . It's
horrible . . . horrible . . .! Oh, God, I feel terrible . . .
violated, used, discarded, utterly rejected, alone and
scared stiff . . . I don't know if I am pregnant or
diseased or needing an abortion or irreparably harmed
. . . I feel sick . . . I want to die . . . How can I face my
family, my friends, myself . . . O God help me to forget
the feeling of utter filth I feel, forget his body on me
and in me. Clean me, O God, in the way only you can.
For if you don't I'll never be clean, never forget, never
forgive. *Never!*

READING

Read a few more books and talk a little less.
Chen Chiju 1558–1639

Read not to contradict and confute, nor to believe and take for granted, nor to find talk and discourse, but to weigh and consider.

Sir Francis Bacon 1561–1626

A book is the best of friends, the same today and for ever.

Martin Farquhar Tupper 1810–1889

Some books are to be tasted, others to be swallowed, and some few to be chewed and digested.

Sir Francis Bacon 1561–1626

Without thought

If a man has read a great number of books and does not think things through, he is only a bookcase.

Shu Shuehmou

The bookful blockhead, ignorantly read,
With loads of learned lumber in his head.

Alexander Pope 1688–1744

REALITY

'What is *real*?' asked the Rabbit one day.

'Real isn't how you are made,' said the Skin Horse.

'It's a thing that happens to you. When a child loves you for a long, long time, not just to play with, but *really* loves you, then you become Real.'

'Does it hurt?' asked the Rabbit.

'Sometimes', said the Skin Horse, for he was always truthful. 'When you are Real you don't mind being hurt.'

'Does it happen all at once, like being wound up,' he asked, 'or bit by bit?'

'It doesn't happen all at once,' said the Skin Horse. 'You become. It takes a long time. That's why it doesn't often happen to people who break easily, or have sharp edges, or who have to be carefully kept. Generally, by the time you are Real, most of your hair has been loved

off, and your eyes drop out and you get loose in the
joints and very shabby. But these things don't matter at
all, because once you are Real you can't be ugly, except
to people who don't understand. Once you are Real it
lasts for always.'

Margery Williams, The Velveteen Rabbit

Is this wall more real than those trees (pointing to the
valley below) because we can touch these stones and
not those branches? Do we need to touch, examine, to
prove that things are real? That tree is beautiful
because it gives us pleasure in its beauty. Do not
search for the creatures in its leaves or the parasites on
its bark or the worms crawling round its roots. The
truth of that tree is in its beauty.

Don Quixote, BBC Productions

REASSURANCE

Now we know God's grace will never cease.
Sometimes we bear pain and suffering
till our hearts are full of darkness.

Father, never from us depart,
keep us poor fold in your kind heart.

God, give grace to us and gladness,
bring us joy despite our sadness.

May mercy be our stay
May your love enlighten each day.

Chao Tzu-Ch'en

Let nothing disturb thee,
Nothing affright thee;
All things are passing;
God never changeth;
Patient endurance
Attaineth to all things;
Who God possesseth
In nothing is wanting;
Alone God sufficeth.

St Teresa of Avila's book-mark

Lord, teach me to be calm and reassured by the nearness of your unfailing presence.

I am a living channel
through which the healthful
currents of life are flowing.
God is my life;
God is my strength;
And in God is my trust.

Lord, help me always to remember everything that is given, and to acknowledge this and be thankful, before I complain.

But now, thus says the Lord, who created you, O Jacob, and he who formed you, O Israel: 'Fear not, for I have redeemed you; I have called you by your name; you are mine. When you pass through the waters, I will be with you; and through the rivers, they shall not overwhelm you. When you walk through the fire you shall not be burned, nor shall the flame scorch you. For I am the Lord your God, The Holy One of Israel, your saviour. Fear not, for I am with you.'

Isaiah 43:1-3f

Loving God and Father of all, in your service we have become old in experience and young in hope. We carry both in the deepest places of our hearts and minds.

We now turn to you with eyes newly open, with hope reawakened, shrugging off the layers of worry and doubt that have closed about us. We are created for your promise, raised for your blessing, fulfilled by your task, and refreshed by worship in your love. Keep us, remember us and make us holy.   Amen.

Sabbath Evening Service, Forms of Prayer for Jewish Worship
(adapted)

Do not think meanly of yourself and do not despair of perfection.

Moses Maimonides 1135–1204

Lord, thou hast been our dwelling place in all
    generations.
Before the mountains were brought forth,
or ever thou hadst formed the earth and the world,
even from everlasting to everlasting, thou art God.

Psalm 90:1-2

'I feel so terrible,' she said waiting to be held. But in
the holding, he could not agree — knowing her need.
    'You look wonderful,' he replied, and meaning it.
    'Yet I feel so awful.'
    'Perhaps,' he responded, 'that is why I am here. Both
of us have will and feelings. But when you feel
something, you may not see that it is not feeling that is
necessary, but fact. And when you *will* something,
perhaps you do not feel as much as you should. It may
be that I am here to share the difference, to speak of it,
and indicate the one, so you may be assured of the
other.'

RECOVERY

Not in the clamour of the crowded street,
Not in the shouts and plaudits of the throng,
But in ourselves, are triumph and defeat.

Henry Wadsworth Longfellow 1807–1882

O God
Help me to live today well,
Help me
    to bear pain, if need be, uncomplainingly,
    and discomfort cheerfully.
Help me
    to cause as little trouble
    and to give as much help as possible.
And help me today
    to take one step forward
    on the road back to health.
This I ask for Jesus' sake.   Amen.

William Barclay, Prayers for Help and Healing

RECONCILIATION, Sacrament of

The sacrament of reconciliation is part of our Lord's warming love expressed through the ministry of healing. Neither of the older terms, confession and penance, conveys a purpose beyond the mechanics of sincere regret and contrition. To confess and yet remain captive to feelings of guilt is to miss the reality of the Church's commission and Christ's command.

Pardon comes through our sincere repentance and our deep desire to put matters right before God and those whom we have wronged. The free flowing power of God's love will only become a reality for us when individually and willingly we confess our sins.

To know how to do this, without wasting emotional energy in self-delusion and being irrelevant, we need the guidance of a spiritual director who will help us to build our lives on three great guidelines, a rule of life suited to our needs, on-going spiritual direction, and regularity in the sacrament of reconciliation. Faithfully followed these will ensure peace of mind and purpose in life, literally becoming saving grace during times of need or stress.

The sacrament of reconciliation has always been public and/or private. In the Anglican Church the guideline has always been, *all may, none must, some should — and many ought.* This is totally confidential and the priest who hears a confession is under a sacred oath never to reveal the contents under any circumstances. Through the proper guidance of a priest the sacrament of reconciliation can be an enormously cleansing experience. Spiritual direction will enable you to discover a deepened awareness about daily living.

Reconciliation commits us to
asking God for discernment to see our sins
being truly sorry
confessing our sins and determining to do better
giving thanks for such cleansing, and fresh
opportunities to do better.

REFORM

A bright future often depends on clearing up a shady
past.   *Chinese aphorism*

REGRET

. . . I was young and foolish, and now am full of tears.
W. B. Yeats 1865–1939, 'Down by the Salley Gardens'

REJECTION

In God's eyes, there is no rejected person.
Lao Tze 604BC

REJOICING

Poor amongst the poor, and aching with compassion
for the misfits and the sinful, Christ nevertheless lived
life as a continuous celebration and wanted to be
remembered as a man with a cup in his hand.
Bishop John Taylor

All the sun long it was running, it was lovely, the hay
Fields high as the house, the tunes from the chimneys,
    it was air
And playing lovely and watery
    And fire green as grass . . .
Under the new made clouds and happy as the heart
    was long,
    In the sun born over and over,
        I ran my heedless ways,
    My wishes raced through the house high hay
And nothing I cared, at my sky blue trades, that time
    allows
In all his tuneful turning so few and such morning
    songs
    Before the children green and golden
        Follow him out of grace.
Dylan Thomas 1914–1953, 'Fern Hill'

RELAXATION

Lord help me now
in yearning and need.
Let me feast with you.
Fill me with the food that endures;
not spiritual snacks
but three-course meals;
not crumbs of prayer
but portions of silence.
And through the busy day
let me relax in you.
Fill my day with spiritual sandwiches
with you at the centre
and activities on either side.
In every action awaken
my inner vision
to see and know
the calming presence
of you.

RELIGION

It is a great mistake to suppose that God is only, or
even chiefly, concerned with religion.

Archbishop William Temple 1881–1944

RELUCTANCE

Reluctance, Lord, is admission that you will not
triumph. Heal my reluctance; fill me with your Spirit;
empower me with your love, now and always.   Amen.

RENEWAL

As a kite needs the wind to fly,
as gloves need hands to be firm,
so I need to be filled, Lord,
with your guiding hand,
your strengthening Spirit
and your redeeming love.   Amen.

REPENTANCE

I cast away any hatred or bitterness that lingers from the week that is past, so that my spirit may be at rest.

Forms of Prayer for Jewish Worship

REPROOF

Frequent reproofs make the friendship distant.

Confucius (K'ung Fu-tze) 551–479BC

RESPECT

Respect a man's life — don't take it.
Respect a man's property — don't steal it.
Respect a man's good name — don't black it.
Respect yourself — don't envy others.
Respect your promises — above all if you make them in God's name.
Love your parents.
Love each other, and be faithful as husband and wife.
Love God above everything.
Set nothing on earth higher than him.

Evan Hooper and Ernest Marvin, A Man Dies

REST

The gathered experience of mankind, that the break in the routine of work one day in seven will heighten the value of the very work itself, is not lightly to be put aside. To dedicate one day a week to rest and to God, this is the prerogative and privilege of man alone.

C. J. G. Montefiore 1858–1938

The day thou gavest, Lord, is ended
    the darkness falls at thy behest;
to thee our morning hymns ascended,
    thy praise shall sanctify our rest.

John Ellerton 1828–1893

Rest and be thankful.

O almighty Father, who, in thy divine mercy, dost cover the earth with the curtain of darkness, that all the weary may rest; grant unto all men rest in thee this night.

Let thy grace, we beseech thee, comfort and support all who are to spend it in sorrow, in anxiety, or in affliction. And we commend unto thy hands all our relations, friends and neighbours. Strengthen and confirm thy faithful people, convert the wicked, arouse the careless, recover the fallen, relieve the sick, give peace to the dying, guide the perplexed and remove all hindrances to the apprehension of thy truth, that thy holy name may be glorified in Jesus Christ, our Lord and saviour. Amen.

Bishop Brooke Foss Westcott 1825–1901

RESTLESSNESS

You have made us, Lord, for yourself, and our heart shall find no rest until it rests in you.

St Augustine of Hippo 354–430

RESPONSIBILITY

Lord of all creation, you have made us to be stewards of the world, to share in partnership with you, and by the guidance of the Holy Spirit, the wonder and true care of all life. Help us each and every day to conserve what is good, encourage what may be better, and in all things to look to you for the wisdom to choose what is right, through Jesus Christ our Lord. Amen.

RESURRECTION

Almighty and everlasting God, whose Son Jesus Christ healed and helped, encouraged and restored people to wholeness,
Lead us from death to life,
   from falsehood to truth;
Lead us from despair to hope;
   from fear to trust;

Lead us from hate to love;
   from war to peace;
Let peace fill our hearts, our world, our universe,
making whole both people and nations through the
ascendant power of the living Christ, even Jesus Christ
our Lord.   Amen.

Anonymous

Easter greeting: Christ is risen.
Response: He is risen indeed.

Traditional

And eternal life
As far as I know there is nothing in the world I am so
sure of, but I have no sort of picture of it and I don't
feel the smallest desire for one. I should know it would
be wrong and therefore I think I am happier without
one.

Archbishop William Temple 1881–1944

Although death comes to us all yet we rejoice in the
promise of eternal life; for to your faithful people life is
changed not taken away; and when our mortal flesh is
laid aside, an everlasting dwelling place is made ready
for us in heaven.

The Alternative Service Book 1980

Heavenly Father,
we give you thanks
because in his victory over the grave
a new age has dawned,
the long reign of sin is ended,
a broken world is being renewed,
and man is once again made whole.

The Alternative Service Book 1980 (adapted)

Heavenly Father,
we give you thanks
because through him

you have given us eternal life
and delivered us from the bondage of sin
and the fear of death
into the glorious liberty of the children of God.

The Alternative Service Book 1980 (adapted)

Mortality is our kindergarten experience, our earliest
conscious knowledge of a life that is not only
everlasting but, more mysterious and wonderful still,
also eternal. Space and time are seeming tyrants but
neither is to be feared for our immortality smiles at
both as we begin to practise it here and await with
reverent curiosity for the wonders that are hidden
behind successive veils of experience of which death is
the last . . . Go on unanxiously with the glad knowledge
that you (and yours) are tied by a bond against which
death is as powerless as is a cloud to extinguish the
sun or a hammer to destroy a moonbeam.

Bishop Charles Henry Brent 1862–1929

For children

Of a waterbug who became a dragonfly

Down below the surface of a quiet pond lived a little
colony of water bugs. They were a happy colony, living
far away from the sun. For many months they were
very busy, scurrying over the soft mud on the bottom
of the pond.

They did not notice that every once in a while one of
their colony seemed to lose interest in going about with
its friends. Clinging to the stem of a pond lily, it
gradually moved out of sight and was seen no more . . .

Finally one of the water bugs, a leader in the colony,
gathered its friends together. 'I have an idea. The next
one of us who climbs up the lily stalk must promise to
come back and tell us where he or she went and why.'
. . .

One spring day, not long after, the very water bug
who had suggested the plan found himself climbing up
the lily stalk. Up, up, up he went. Before he knew what

was happening, he had broken through the surface of the water, and fallen on to the broad, green lily pad above. When he awoke, he looked about with surprise. He couldn't believe what he saw. A startling change had come to his old body. His movement revealed four silver wings and a long tail . . .

The dragonfly remembered the promise: 'The next one of us who climbs up the lily stalk will come back and tell where he or she went and why.'

Without thinking, the dragonfly darted down. Suddenly he hit the surface of the water and bounced away. Now that he was a dragonfly he could no longer go into the water.

'I can't return!' he said in dismay. 'At least I tried, but I can't keep my promise. Even if I could go back, not one of the water bugs would know me in my new body. I guess I'll just have to wait until they become dragonflies too. Then they'll understand what happened to me, and where I went.'

And the dragonfly winged off happily into its wonderful new world of sun and air.

Doris Stickney

Conversation between a priest and a 5 year old girl.

Girl: *(playing with her old ragged doll; after a long discussion, there is a silence)* And so God made the special bit which is inside each of us. And he loves that special bit for ever and because he wanted to see what we look like he gave us bodies with flesh and bones. And because we live in a cold climate we have to have clothes.

Priest: Yes.

Girl: And then, like my dolly when it wears out we have to get rid of the body which is either put in the ground or burnt — otherwise there'd be bodies lying all over the place.

Priest: Yes.

Girl: And the body is like a shell that wears out, but the special bit goes back to God who loves our special bit for ever and ever.

Priest: Yes that's right.
Girl: (pause) You know something?
Priest: What?
Girl: God's very neat, isn't he?

A spider spun a silken thread
And swung from grass to ground
'I must find out the news,' he said
'That's buzzing all around.'
The garden creatures great and small
Were quiet as a mouse,
They saw the caterpillar crawl
Into a tiny house.
'He's such a fool,' said the ladybird
As she polished up her nails.
'It's the silliest thing I've ever heard,'
Said a pair of solemn snails.
So all the creatures went away
All thinking she was dead
Until one bright and lovely day
A little earthworm said
'I see a crack in the little shell
And something moves inside
I see a head and wings as well
Come quick and see,' she cried.
'The caterpillar's back,' they said.
Before their very eyes
A butterfly stepped out
And smiled at their surprise.
'I left the life you thought I knew.
You thought that I was dead.
I did it just to show to you
We die to grow,' she said.

Author unknown

There is a vivid lesson to be learned from the butterfly.
    The first thing the larva does when it is born is to eat
its own casing, then it wraps itself in its own
substance, in its past, and hangs suspended in the

present, motionless, in the darkness, with all the appearance of being useless, while its wings are growing.

When it has developed fully, it breaks out of its cocoon and spreads its wings so that the sun may bring out the full beauty of their colours. There, at the butterfly's feet, lies its second winding sheet, its second shroud, a silent symbol of the past. What will the butterfly do with it? Just fly off and leave it? Or use it as a waste-basket? Or keep it as a family heirloom in a moss-lined nest? Actually, it does none of these things. Once again it eats the casing it has cast off, and having done so, it sets out on its beautiful wings to conquer new worlds.

The butterfly literally eats its own past as a sacred symbol of respect and gratitude. The past is incorporated into its present life. And that past, which it did not despise but rather absorbed and made part of its living body, serves as the essential link between two worlds that must always join hands, the past and the present. The butterfly does not collect souvenirs of the past because it actually swallows up its past, and so it will not fall into the temptation of abandoning its flight to settle down in front of its cast-off cocoon, and perhaps tired with flying so far, remain to mourn its former life as a placid, chubby caterpillar.

Juan Arias, on how we should deal with the past and with
change

RETURNING

Lord my life has been like a house with shutters up, curtains drawn, doors closed.

Your knock at the door of my life has bid me open the shutters, the curtains, the door, and step out with you into the fresh air and the open world.

I blamed you, Lord, as I stood in your presence, facing the darkness and seeing nothing, which I thought was you. So I blamed you, I hated you, I despaired continually and on my face at work, and with friends, wore the mask of disapproval and unresolved fear.

Then, very gently, you tapped me on the shoulder, as would a most loving friend, caught my eye, and turned me around so that I could see your light and move more surely into your presence.

REVELATION

With my faith
I reach out for the switch
in the dark

With my hope
I feel for it there
in the dark

With my love
I know that it is there
in the dark

Then my faith
was sorely tested
in the dark

And my hope was soon depleted
in the dark

And my love
was shrivelled slowly
in the dark

for the bulb had gone
the fuse had blown
the flex had snapped
and the socket rattled
in the dark

Then I remembered
The matches in my pocket
in the dark.

O everlasting Father, who has brought nations to your
light and kings to the brightness of your rising, fill, we
beseech you, our whole creation with your glory and
show yourself unto all the peoples of the earth, through
him who is the true light that enlightens everyone that
comes into the world, even your son Jesus Christ.

Traditional

I said to the almond tree,
'Speak to me of God.'
And the almond tree blossomed.

Anonymous

And what is this? I asked the earth and it said, 'I am
not he,' and whatsoever is in it confessed the same. I
asked the sea and the deeps, and all that swimming or
creeping live therein, and they answered, 'We are not
thy God, seek above us.'

I asked the wandering winds; and the whole air with
its inhabitants spoke, 'I am not God.' I asked the
heavens, sun, moon and stars. 'Nor,' said they, 'are we
the God whom thou seekest.' And I replied, 'Ye have
told me of my God, that ye are not he; 'tell me
something of him.' And they cried all with a great
voice, 'He made us.' And their beauty was my answer.

St Augustine of Hippo 354–430

Christ is the head of this institution,
The invisible doctor near every bed,
The unseen inspector of every work,
The silent listener to every conversation,
The quiet sympathiser and comforter
  in every pain and sorrow.

From the noticeboard at Tarn Taran Leprosy Hospital in the
Punjab

The world is charged with the grandeur of God.

Gerard Manley Hopkins 1844–1889, 'God's Grandeur'

SACRAMENTS

Love is a sacrament that should be taken kneeling, and
Lord, I am not worthy should be on the lips and in the
hearts of those who receive it.

Oscar Wilde 1854–1900 (adapted)

The sacraments are free-flowing channels of God's
grace. They imply commitment and are mysteries that
disclose themselves only to those who believe. Each
sacrament bears an outward sign of an inner and holy
reality which sanctifies the recipient. The sacraments
are administered by bishops, priests or deacons, and
consist of:

Anointing	**M**arriage
Baptism	**O**rdination
Confirmation	**R**econciliation
	Eucharist

Christianity is essentially sacramental. Christ, by his
incarnation, showed that matter is capable of revealing
God's truth and grace. The world, other people and we
ourselves are essentially sacramental. There are
sacraments for every occasion.

We can and should ask for the sacraments, for
example when we are happy (as with an anniversary,
birthday, specially joyous occasion, by anointing) or
when housebound (as with the eucharist) or when sick
or severely ill (possibly both of these sacraments).
Prayer and sacraments go hand in hand. Not nearly
enough use is made of anointing as a means of
affirming God's great love for us through his warm and
redeeming nature. As we receive medicines for the
body, so we ought even more so to receive sacraments
for the soul.

The sacramental hand of God has two main thumbs
(baptism and eucharist) and five lesser fingers. Like a
hand, the more the sacraments touch our lives the more
loved we feel, and therefore can give, share, enjoy and
fulfil.

My lord and my saviour support me in the strong arms
of thy sacraments.

John Henry Newman 1801–1890

SACRIFICE

Sacrifice consists in giving up something at personal
cost; for example, the surgeon who gives up gardening
to preserve the sensitivity of his hands, or the water-
tasters of London who swear never to drink alcohol.

See also John 3:16, 3:30, 10:11, 15:12-13; Luke 15:31f,
17:10, 19:8, 22:42, 23:46; Mark 1:38, 5:30, 8:35-36, 10:29-
30, 10:45.

SANCTITY (of the body)

Lord, there she was, standing in the foyer of the
    strip-joint, with a gem stone in her navel.
Embedded in that scar denoting life's beginning
    and I felt ashamed.
For, somehow I realised that we have become a
    people absorbed in the cult of the body.
Walk with me, Lord, along the brightly lighted
    street just here.
    Look, Lord, with pity and weep.
Lovely girls, exposed to the lusts of men,
    besmirching all that's fair and feminine.
    Where are we headed, Lord?
Then suddenly, I saw another body and another
    time.
A body nailed to a tree.
    That body broken because
    All bodies are precious to you.
Teach me, O Lord, the sanctity of the individual.
    And to care, even as you cared.   Amen.

Roger Bush

SANITY

If you can keep your head when all about you
Are losing theirs . . .

Rudyard Kipling 1865–1936, 'If —'

Lord thank you for the gift of sanity, with clear
thinking, calm reflection; deep appreciation and an
increasing awareness of you.   Amen.

SCARS

They injured her body but they scalded her mind.
Japanese

Though the body heals the scars remain — as
reminders.

Lord though I have been wounded and though I bear
pain, let the scars remain my scars and give me the
gentleness and bearing of your loving spirit.   Amen.

SEASONS, The

It is always springtime in a soul that loves God.
St Jean-Baptiste Marie Vianney (the Curé d'Ars) 1786–1859

Now is the winter of our discontent
Made glorious summer . . .
William Shakespeare 1564–1616, Richard III

You are there on the heights, Lord
surveying the land, the cities and fields;
You are there in the depths, Lord
sharing the gloom, the despair and doubt;
You are there in my heart, Lord
clearing the dross for spaces of love;
You are here in my soul, Lord
preparing the way through pains to joy:
But most of all, Lord, you are here.

Lord of the wilderness in springtime,
conqueror of temptation, pain and death,
Let me ever hold fast to you.
Lent discipline

SEEING

Lord, open my eyes so that I do not merely see but
truly perceive.   Amen.

Thank you Father for the wonderful gift of sight. Help
me never to take something so precious for granted;
and make me truly sympathetic to all whose sight is
impaired, especially those who are blind.   Amen.

Blind man on cultivating his garden

I feel my way round. I can touch my flowers and
shrubs. I can smell their fragrance. I can delight others,
and they can stop and chat with me. All that means
something to a blind man.

Seeing again

I had waited for the first eye operation with some
apprehension.

Now it was the same again — why? The last
experience had resulted in a miracle of restored sight.
Then why be afraid?

Losing consciousness — going into the dark — if
only it could all happen without that 'letting go'! Here
was the trolley and soon I was in the anaesthetic room
— everyone very cheerful — and, 'I'm just giving you a
little prick in your wrist and one, two, thr . . .'

'Surely darkness will steal over me; night will close
around me.' And so into the darkness that had to be
before any healing could begin. Only when I was not
feeling pain and was totally relaxed could God work
this healing through the infinite skill of the surgeon
and his team.

I had 'let go', despite all the fears, into the darkness
that God needs, the darkness in which to work his
healing.

'Darkness is no darkness for thee and night is
luminous as day — to thee both dark and light are as
one' — and so the second miracle happened!

Jo Lapage

Thank you Lord for calling me out of the darkness into your marvellous light; light that has been there all the time, like your constant love for me — but now my eyes are opening and I can see light, pouring through the new crystal lens into my eyes with all the sparkling clearness of a winter dawn — painful at first in its brilliance; light, in which all the myriad colours of the rainbow bring to life the wonderful detail of your creation: the tiny hairs on the leaf, the beauty in the veins of the petal, the texture of the old clothes, now each fibre vibrant with colour.

But most of all the faces of all the people around me. I had to feel the darkness, Lord, to know this wonder of your light.

Jo Lapage

SEEKING

Lord, where shall I find you?
High and hidden is your place.
And where shall I not find you?
The world is full of your glory.

I have sought your nearness,
With all my heart I called you
And going out to meet you
I found you coming to meet me.

Judah Halem

SELF-CENTREDNESS

A human being cannot be brought into harmony with absolute reality unless he can get rid of innate self-centredness. This is the hardest task that man can set himself.

Arnold Toynbee 1889–1975

It would be very singular that in nature, all the planets should obey eternal laws and that there should be a little animal 5 feet high who, in contempt of these laws, could act as he pleased solely according to his caprice.

Voltaire 1694–1778

SELF-CONTROL

When the passions have once been indulged, they cannot be easily restrained.

Chinese aphorism

SELF-EXAMINATION

Re-examine all you have been told, at school, church or in any book, and dismiss whatever insults your own soul.

Walt Whitman 1819–1892

SELFISHNESS

One-way love keeps two from ever being one.

Robert Vavra, The Love of Tiger Flower

All sufferings,
All injustices, bitterness, humiliations, griefs,
   hates, despairs,
All sufferings are an unappeased hunger,
A hunger for love,
So men have built, slowly, selfishness by selfishness,
   a disfigured world that crushes them;
So the men on earth spend their time feeding their
   self-love,
While around them others with outstretched arms die
   of hunger.
They have squandered your love, Lord.
Help me to love, Lord,
not to waste my powers of love,
to love myself less and less in order to love others
   more and more,
that around me, no one should suffer or die because
   I have stolen the love they needed to live.

Michel Quoist

SELF-KNOWLEDGE

You never know yourself till you know more than your

body. The image of God is not sealed in the features of your face, but in the lineaments of your soul.

Thomas Traherne 1637–1674

SELFLESSNESS

Leaping with joy to any task for others.

Franciscan women working at Woolwich

See also Selfishness

SELF-SURRENDER

Into your hands I commend my spirit. Your will, not mine, be done.

Jesus Christ

No man can do properly what he is called upon to do in this life unless he can learn to forget his ego and act as an instrument of God.

W. H. Auden 1907–1973

Father, I abandon myself into your hands; do with me what you will.

Whatever you may do, I thank you; I am ready for all, I accept all. Let only your will be done in me, and in all your creatures — I wish no more than this, O Lord.

Jesus Caritas

There's but one gift that all our dead desire;
One gift that men can give — and that's a dream
Unless we too can burn with that same fire
Of sacrifice, die to the things that seem,
Die to the little hatreds, die to greed,
Die to the old ignoble selves that once we knew,
Die to the base contempts of sect and creed,
And rise, again like these, with souls as true.
And that's not done by sword, or tongue, or pen.
There's but one way. God make us better men.

Tubby Clayton 1885–1972

God will not ask thy name;
Nor will he seek thy birth;
Alone will he demand of thee
What thou hast done on earth.

Anonymous

Unlike men's frontiers
God' frontiers may be crossed without permit or
    passport.
There is a frontier I may cross
deep within my own heart.
There is a frontier I may cross
as I reach out in loving concern to another man's need.
Always I live on the frontier.

Congregational Prayer Fellowship

O my God, I am not my own but yours; take me for
    your own;
make me in all things
to do your will.
O my God, I give myself to you for joy or for sorrow,
for sickness or for health, for life or for death, for time
    or for eternity.
Make me and keep me always your own, for Jesus
    Christ's sake.   Amen.

The Methodist Service Book

I am no longer my own, but yours. Put me to do what
you will, rank me with whom you will; put me to
doing, put me to suffering; let me be employed for you
or laid aside for you, exalted for you or brought low for
you; let me be full, let me be empty; let me have all
things, let me have nothing; I freely and
wholeheartedly yield all things to your pleasure and
your disposal. And now, glorious and blessed God,
Father, Son and Holy Spirit, you are mine and I am
yours. So be it. And the covenant now made on earth,
let it be ratified in heaven.   Amen.

The Methodist Covenant Service

Lord of truth and mercy, we pray to thee to take away
our selfishness and give us your holiness;
our indifference and give us your zeal;
our smallness and make us generous;
our thirst for recognition and make us
    thirst for righteousness.

Prayer of the United Church of North India

Bear the burden of one another's failings; then you will
be fulfilling the law of Christ.

Galatians 6:2

He passed by on the road;
They pressed him into service,
The first to come along, a stranger.
Lord, you accepted his help . . .
By your own choosing you are in need of us.
Lord, I need others.
The way of man is too hard to be trodden alone.
But I avoid the hands outstretched to help me,
I want to act alone,
I want to fight alone,
I want to succeed alone.

And yet beside me walk a friend, a spouse, a brother,
    a neighbour, a fellow-worker.
You have placed them near me, Lord, and too often I
    ignore them.
And yet it is together that we shall save the world.

Lord even if they are requisitioned, grant that I may
see, that I may accept, all the Simons on my road.

Michel Quoist

To pity your sufferings and the sufferings of the world
    I manage very well, Lord,
But to weep for my own sins, that's another matter.

Michel Quoist

Whenever a man feels called upon to neglect his natural interest or his animal desires in the service of any sort of ideal whatsoever, there you have the movement of the Holy Spirit.

Archbishop William Temple 1881–1944

Grant, O God,
that we may never lose the way through our self-will,
and so end up in the far countries of the soul;
that we may never abandon the struggle
but that we may endure to the end,
and so be saved;
that we may never drop out of the race,
but that we may ever press forward
to the goal of our high calling;
that we may never choose the cheap and passing
   things,
and let go the precious things that last for ever;
that we may never take the easy way,
and so leave the right way;
that we may never forget
that sweat is the price of all things,
and that without the cross, there cannot be the crown.

Catholic Prayer Book

Of a priest

O God help me to worship you only, and to lose myself in you. Help me not to put my trust in my own efforts. Save me from winning men for myself, for a system or for a formula. Teach me to be humble, and to forswear, like you, all attempts to compel men to believe.

Teach me how to pull down the shutters of my mind so that I am not overwhelmed by a multiplicity of confused concerns. In my creation give me the order and planning of yours, and help me to balance my vocations to the priesthood and to marriage.

Howard Hammerton, A Pastoral Medley

SENSITIVITY

Lord thank you for my sensitivity, that enables gentleness and perceptiveness.

How wonderful you are to give me and all your people such a precious gift. Teach me to develop this gift wisely. Too little and I will be unaware of important and necessary values and needs. Too much and I will be an immature slave to myself. Lord, guide me with *your* sensitivity in the right way, for Jesus' sake. Amen.

Feel the tribulations of the individual and of the multitude, and implore God to ease their burden.

Nachman of Bratzlav 1772–1811

SEPARATION

Entreat me not to leave you, for wherever you go I will go; and wherever you lodge, I will lodge; your people shall be my people, and your God, my God. Where you die, I will die, and there will I be buried. The Lord do so to me, and more also, if anything but death parts you and me.

Ruth 1:16-17

See also Psalm 137, Hosea 11:1-4, 8-9, II Samuel 1:19-27, John 17:20-21, Luke 24:30-31

Lo, I am with you always even to the end of time.

Matthew 28:20

SEXUAL LOVE

Sexual love ought to contain an immense amount of liking. We ought to be married to the kind of person we like enormously.

J. B. Priestley 1894–1984

In perspective

Here I am God, as you designed me. Sin and disobedience to your instructions may have upset the balance of things, but I need to love and to be loved.

Show me the way through which all this energy can be redirected, and then teach me to laugh at myself for getting things out of proportion. To laugh at sex helps to scale down its importance.

Margaret Evening, Who Walks Alone

Cravings of the senses deplete your inner peace.

SHAME

The sense of shame is of great importance to a man.

Mencius (Meng-K'o) 372–289BC

Your neglect is my shame.

SHARING

Lord keep me from private-mindedness. In order to create an atmosphere of brotherhood, give me each day a happy temper, a friendly mind and a generous heart.

Bishop Charles Henry Brent 1862–1929 (adapted)

The joy of going through life hand in hand with the comrade of one's choice, sharing one another's burdens, stimulating one another's courage, doubling one another's sagacity, and easing one another's pain.

W. C. Willoughby, Race Problems and the New Africa

SICKNESS

The Lord is near, have no anxiety, but in everything make your requests known to God in prayer and petition with thanksgiving.   *Philippians 4:6*

God himself has said, 'I will never leave you or desert you.'   *Hebrews 13:5*

Lord help and hold me in your great power to bear this pain and illness in that strength which your cross and passion gives through Jesus Christ.   Amen.

The minister is to be sent for not while the case is
desperate, but before the sickness is come to its crisis.

Bishop Jeremy Taylor 1613–1667

SIDE-EFFECTS

Father help all those who are suffering from side-
effects. Let those who discover, distribute and prescribe
medicines be truly careful, considerate and responsible
in what they do.

Let no drugs be deliberately given to perpetuate
adverse symptoms, and enable those who pioneer
safeguards to maintain their vigilance and
skill.   Amen.

SILENCE

And in your nothingness and silence love is born
And in your footsteps even desert land will flower
And in silence that is yours the heavens open
And the long awaited song of love is heard
Now and through all eternity.

Anonymous

If your words are no better than silence, keep silent.

Lord help me to remember that silence is healing.

Let silence speak in its own time, its own way,
unhurried by desire, untrammelled by confusion.
Let silence speak, to affirm or point to other things,
from the gift which only silence brings.

SIMPLICITY

Begin praying simply — when glad
                      — when distressed
                      — when exhausted

SIN

Ways of sinning

The seven deadly sins	*Opposites*	*The seven great virtues*
Covetousness	Generosity	Faith
Lust	Chastity	Hope
Anger	Patience	Charity
Sloth	Diligence	Courage
Pride	Humility	Temperance
Envy	Charity	Prudence
Greed (gluttony)	Temperance	Justice

The seven deadly sins
1 Politics without principles.
2 Wealth without work.
3 Pleasure without conscience.
4 Knowledge without character.
5 Commerce without morality.
6 Worship without sacrifice.
7 Science without humanity.

Mahatma Gandhi 1868–1948

Modern sins
The two great modern sins are ingratitude and indifference. Am I guilty of these?

If so Lord, from this moment make me thankful, sensitive and caring.   Amen.

Fighting sin
Because sin spoils, disturbs our peace, and needs the will to put things right, it is vital to say sorry by confessing faults, and asking sincerely for forgiveness so as to confer peace and love.

The nine fruits of the spirit are love, joy, peace, patience, kindness, goodness, faithfulness, gentleness, self-control.

Galatians 5:22

Rank and reward have no appeal for a man at one with himself. A man truly himself will not enrich his own interests and make a virtue of poverty. He goes his way without depending on others; yet, is not arrogant that he needs no one. The greatest man is nobody.

Chinese

Before you can be filled you must first be empty. Empty the vessel so the vessel may be filled with holy poverty, with the Spirit that is pure.

I want you to choose freely, I want you to be able to decide what to do and what not to do. If you choose what is good you will receive my joy and peace.

Sirach 17:1-11

There is no guilt greater than to sanction unbridled ambition. No calamity greater than to be satisfied with one's lot. No fault greater than the wish to be continually receiving. *Lao Tze b. 604BC*

Once when crossing high mountains the *Sadhu, Sundar Singh, was caught in a snowstorm. Frozen corpses littered the way. The wind grew fiercer, the snow more deep. As he crouched and struggled forward he was joined by a Tibetan who feared to journey alone to Ranget. From time to time the wind abated, only to blow again with renewed strength. They began to despair of reaching the village which was far ahead.

Suddenly, as they rounded a steep slope they saw, about thirty feet below, the body of a man lying unconscious. The Sadhu asked his companion to help pull the man up so that they could take him to the village. Fool, said the Tibetan, if you pause you too will die; I will save myself. And he journeyed on. The Sadhu found to his dismay that the fallen man was still

* 'Holy man'. Sadhu Sundar Singh was converted to Christianity. He never wore even sandals.

alive. Gradually he dragged the snow-covered body up to the pathway. Very slowly and very carefully he helped carry the man forward along the dangerous track.

So great was the exertion that, in spite of the intense cold, eventually the Sadhu began to perspire; in turn, the warmth of the Sadhu's body began to revive the man. On and on they trudged in the storm until, within sight of the village, the sky began to clear. And there, on the trail ahead, lay a mound that was heavily covered with snow. It was the body of the Tibetan.

See also Luke 10:25f, Mark 10:45, Isaiah 53:4f, John 1:29, 3:21.

SINGLE, Being

All false notions must be swept away if single people are to look upon their way of life as quite as satisfactory and fulfilling as that of marriage.

Margaret Evening, Who Walks Alone

SINGLE-HOMELESS, The

Lord, you had nowhere to lay your head, no home to call your own. Be the strength, support and care of all who are single-homeless, and guide them in times of difficulty and despair, through Jesus Christ our Lord.   Amen.

Lord, let your resilient spirit sustain all who care for the single-homeless. Let the bonds of friendship and the gift of hospitality be strengthened as their care increases; for Jesus' sake.   Amen.

SLEEP

The debt we pay to sleep is the credit we receive the following day.

Good luck to him who invented sleep . . . that makes
the shepherd with the king and the fool with the wise
man.

> *Miguel de Cervantes 1547–1616,*
> *Sancho Panza in* Don Quixote

The Lord provides for those he loves, while they are
asleep.

> *Psalm 127:1*

Lord, before I go to sleep I want to give thanks for the
blessings of the day, all I have learnt, all I have shared,
everything that has been given as insights to your love
and wisdom for my days. Amen.

Cause us, our Father, to lie down in peace and rise
again to enjoy life.
> *Daily Evening Service, Forms of Prayer for Jewish Worship*

SLEEPLESSNESS

Endless is the watch of the sleepless, Lord. Desperation
is often close at hand. Be instead, Lord, their
watchfulness and their peace, that they may find in you
the ease to let go, the means to their peace, and the
blessing of longed-for sleep; through Jesus Christ our
Lord. Amen.

SMILE, The value of a

It costs nothing but creates much. It enriches those who
receive it, without impoverishing those who give it. It
happens in a flash and the memory of it sometimes
lasts forever. None are so rich that they can get along
without it and none are so poor that they are not richer
for a smile. It creates happiness in the home, fosters
good will in a business and it is the countersign of
friends. It is rest to the weary, daylight to the
discouraged, sunshine to the sad and nature's best
antidote for trouble. Yet it cannot be bought, begged,

borrowed or stolen, for it is something that is of no
earthly good to anyone until it is given away. And if it
ever happens that some people should be too tired to
give you a smile, why not leave one of yours? For
nobody needs a smile so much as one who has no
smile to give.

Property Magazine

SOCIAL SERVICES

Bless all the people who serve our needs —
Butchers and bakers, greengrocers and milkmen;
Postmen and bus-drivers and conductors;
Garbage-collectors and policemen;
Librarians and artists and songwriters;
And the very many more who never fail us.   Amen.

Rita Snowden

SOLITARINESS

One solitary life

He was born in an obscure village, the child of a
peasant woman. He grew up in still another village,
where he worked in a carpenter's shop until he was
thirty. Then he became an itinerant preacher. He never
wrote a book. He never held an office. He never had a
family or owned a house. He didn't go to college. He
never visited a big city. He never travelled two
hundred miles from where he was born. He did none
of the things one usually associates with greatness.

He had no credentials but himself. He was only in
his thirties when the tide of public opinion turned
against him. His friends ran away. He was turned over
to his enemies and went through the mockery of a trial.
He was nailed to a cross between two thieves. While he
was dying, his executioners gambled for his clothing,
the only property he had on earth. When he was dead,
he was laid in a borrowed grave through the pity of a
friend. Nineteen centuries have come and gone, and
today he is the central figure of the human race and the

leader of mankind's progress.

All the armies that ever marched, all the navies that ever sailed, all the parliaments that ever sat, and all the kings that ever reigned, have not affected the life of man on this earth as much as that one solitary life.

Author unknown

I am alone and I want to be two.
I speak, and no one is there to listen.
I live, and no one is there to share my life.

Michel Quoist

The hunchback in the park
A solitary mister
Propped between trees and water
From the opening of the garden lock
That lets the trees and the water enter
Until the Sunday sombre bell at dark.

Dylan Thomas 1914–1953, 'The Hunchback in the Park'

'Why are you so sad?' said the West Wind to the Birch Tree.

'Alas I am so useless,' said the beautiful Birch, 'I cannot bear fruit like the cherry and the apple. Why even the potato is useful, and the dumpy turnip. Now I shall be of no use till I am cut down and made into furniture and sold as a bedroom suite. If I could only bear cherries, or currants or gooseberries.'

'Ha! Ha!' laughed the West Wind, 'I have just heard the apple grumbling, the cherry wailing, the potato and the turnip complaining.

'They all have their complaints. But I'll tell you something about love and yourself.

'There's a man who comes out of the city. Nearly every day he comes like one who is bearing a burden, till he comes to the edge of the wood where he can see *you*. Then he raises his eyes and they suddenly fill with sunlight. So he goes back brightened and cheered because of who you are, and not what you do.'

H. Bellyse Baildon (adapted)

SORENESS

Ease the pain and soreness, Lord, of all who spend long hours in discomfort. Be their strengthening, their patience, their fortitude and their trust.   Amen.

SORROW

The deeper that sorrow carves into your being, the more joy you can contain. Joy and sorrow are inseparable.

Kahlil Gibran 1883–1931

SOUL

There is power in the human soul, said the Lord, when you break through and set it free. Like the power of the atom, more powerful than the atom. It can control the atom, the only thing in the world that can.

I told you that the atom is the greatest force in the world, save one. That is the human soul.

Hermann Hagedorn, cf Deuteronomy 6:4-5

SPEAKING

Speak of men's virtues as if they were your own, and of their vices as if you were liable to their punishment.

Mencius (Meng-K'o) 372–289BC

My God, keep my tongue from causing harm, and my lips from telling lies. Let me be silent if people curse me, my soul still humble and at peace with all. Open my heart to your teaching, and give me the will to practise it. May the plans and schemes of those who seek my harm come to nothing. May the words of my mouth and the meditation of my heart be acceptable to you, O Lord, my rock and my redeemer.

Daily Amidah (Standing Prayer)
Forms of Prayer for Jewish Worship

Because someone speaks with a foreign accent it does not mean that they are deaf.

Speak clearly to the deaf
slowly with the pained
quietly to the tender
And listen to their need.

People do not remember much of what you say. But they do remember how you said it. Hence the great importance of how you say hello and how you say goodbye: the one sets the tone of the conversation, the other the quality of what is remembered.

Rules

Golden Rule

Is it kind?
Is it necessary?
Is it true?

Some dos

1 If you can find nothing at all to say, don't say it.
2 Always know what you mean to say.
3 Arrange your remarks in some sort of order.
4 At all times be clear.
5 Reflect on the kind of audience you have.
6 Never despise those whom you address.
7 Be sparing of literary ornament.
8 Beware of abusing humorous stories.
9 Never be dull. It is better to be flippant than to be dull.

The Don'ts

1 Don't profess undue modesty.
2 Don't dawdle at the outset.
3 Don't drag in a story unless it fully illustrates the point.
4 'Don't strew your pathway with dreadful 'ers'' (Oliver Wendell Holmes).
5 Don't say you will not speak for long.
6 Watch those to whom you are speaking.

Lord Bryce

STILLNESS

At the still point of the turning world. Neither flesh
   nor fleshless;
Neither from nor towards; at the still point, there
   the dance is,
But neither arrest nor movement. And do not call it
   fixity,
Where past and future are gathered. Neither movement
   from nor towards,
Neither ascent nor decline. Except for the point, the still
   point,
There would be no dance, and there is only the dance.

T. S. Eliot 1888–1965, 'Burnt Norton'

STRAIN

To let the anger come out is no bad thing. For so often
diseases of strain and depression are caused by
supressed anger and hatred of other people or oneself.
So it is healthy that it should come out — and God can
take it.

Bishop John Robinson 1919–1983

STRENGTH

There is a strength in us which comes from a strong
and disciplined body. There is another strength that
allows us to feel the pain of others, and give comfort
where comfort is needed. This comes from a
compassionate heart. True strength must combine both.

Chinese

Any man can be broken — by a strength outside
greater than himself or a weakness inside which he
cannot understand.
   Do you forget that your spirit is stronger than the
flesh? It can defeat the power of another, no matter
how great. There is no pain, no defeat, no weakness
within you: only that which you allow to settle in your
own mind. Draw upon the strength of your spirit.

Chinese

There are two kinds of strength, the outer strength is obvious — it fades with age and succumbs to sickness. Then there is the inner strength: to achieve that is much more difficult to develop. The inner strength lasts through every heat and every cold, through old age and . . . beyond.

Chinese

Avoid rather than check,
Check rather than hurt.
Hurt rather that maim.
Maim rather than kill.
For all life is precious;
Nor can any be replaced.

Chinese

The eternal God is your dwelling-place and underneath are the everlasting arms.

Deuteronomy 34:27

O God, stay with me; let
no word cross my lips
that is not your word;
no thoughts enter my mind
that are not your thoughts;
no deed ever done or entertained by me
that is not your deed.

Malcolm Muggeridge, Jesus Rediscovered

SUCCESS

Forget not your failures in your moment of success.

Chinese

SUFFERING

The suffering person just wants the Christ in you to be there.

There is that within each of us which must be
overcome before we can safely face the world.

Bishop Brooke Foss Westcott 1825–1901

Measure thy life by loss instead of gain,
Not by wine drunk, but the wine poured forth.

Harriet King

'There! Didn't I always tell you there must be a God
like that?'

*An old Chinese scholar's comment on hearing for the first
time the story of the cross*

Christ leads me through no darker rooms than those
which he himself went through before.

Richard Baxter 1615–1691

O Jerusalem
Ten measures of beauty came into the world
Jerusalem took nine and the rest of the world one.
There are ten measures of suffering in the world
Nine in Jerusalem and one in the rest of the world.

The Jewish Sages

In poverty and
  simplicity
In brokenness and
  humility
You came for
  me.

A prayer of thanksgiving

Thanks be to thee O Lord Jesus Christ, for all the
benefits which thou hast given us; for all the pains and
insults which thou has borne for us.

O most merciful redeemer, friend and brother, may
we know thee more clearly, love thee more dearly, and
follow thee more nearly.

St Richard, Bishop of Chichester 1245–1253

Without wounds
We would be too strong;
Without his love
We are too weak.

What makes the desert beautiful is that somewhere, far
below its surface, it holds a spring of fresh water.
Antoine de Saint-Exupéry 1900–1944, The Little Prince

Know how sublime a thing it is
to suffer and be strong.
Henry Wadsworth Longfellow 1807–1882

SUICIDE (of a monk)

Everyone loved him . . . Why did he take his own life?
The *yes* and the *no*. In him the *no* conquered. Perhaps
he looked down into our valley knowing that soon he
would have to leave it. But instead of the beauty we
observe, he saw ugliness.
When he looked down into our valley and saw
ugliness, he did not like what he revealed. He saw
ugliness where nothing exists but a valley.

Chinese

SUSPICION

Suspect a man, and he will soon merit your suspicion.
Tubby Clayton 1885–1972

SYMPATHY

And whoever walks a furlong without sympathy walks
to his own funeral drest in a shroud.
Walt Whitman 1819–1892

Lord give me every gentleness and every tenderness,
every insight and every care to bring your sympathy to
others.   Amen.

TEARS

Tears are not enough for you, Lord,
who are the smile of the morning;
for the pain is in the oneness;
the oneness in the sharing;
and in the sharing love
smiles again
with you.

Thank you Lord for the cleansing power of tears, tears
through anguish, tears through grief, tears of ecstatic
joy.   Amen.

Tears, idle tears, I know not what they mean,
Tears from the depth of some divine despair,
Rise in the heart, and gather to the eyes.

Alfred, Lord Tennyson 1809–1892

When bereaved

Help me, Lord, to cry when the feeling comes, so that
in venting my emotion, healing may come.   Amen.

TELEPHONE

You did not call a single time;
It left me all deflated.
If you had only called me once
I would have been elated.

It's funny how a simple thing
Like calling on the phone
Can make one feel important and
Not just so much alone.

Anonymous

I have just hung up; why did he telephone?
I don't know . . . Oh! I get it . . .
I talked a lot and listened very little.

Forgive me, Lord, it was a monologue and not a
    dialogue.
I explained my idea and did not get his;
Since I didn't listen, I learned nothing,
Since I didn't listen, I didn't help,
Since I didn't listen, we didn't communicate.

Forgive me, Lord, for we were connected,
and now we are cut off.

Michel Quoist

TEMPTATION

How special can a relationship be without falling into
    error?
Not so special that any other friend is neglected or
    considered a nuisance.
Not so special that one can really only enjoy the times
    when one is alone with that person.
Not so special that jealousy creeps in.
Not so special that one is constantly living memories,
    or eagerly anticipating meetings of the future, never
    able to enjoy to the full what J. P. de Caussade has
    called 'the sacrament of the present moment'.
Never so special that the prospect of separation at some
    future date is like a sword of Damocles hanging over
    that friendship.
Not so special that it affects normal relationships with
    the opposite sex.
Not so inseparable that the two lives become
    inseparably intertwined.

Margaret Evening, Who Walks Alone

To reassure the flower, you do not have to keep
    plucking it:
check the soil, encourage the sunlight, be constant in
    care.

In a triangular relationship

A woman enmeshed in a relationship with a married man wrote:

I prayed constantly —
  that the love should be hallowed;
  that it would make me more loving towards others;
  that we should be preserved from adultery;
  that his wife and children should not be hurt;
  that there should never be any scandal;
  that we should not abuse the gift of love
  which we felt sure was given by God.

  Margaret Evening, Who Walks Alone

TENDERNESS

Only the truly strong can be tender. And the tender mercy of God leads into the way of peace.

TENSION

Lord, if I am tense
how close am I to you?
If I am tense,
why do I not radiate
your quiet confidence
and abiding love?
Give me, Lord, the honesty
to answer these questions.

  When did I last get three nights' adequate sleep?
  When did the order of my priorities become
    unbalanced?
  When did I last examine my life carefully?
  Do I need to improve relationships?
  Do I see enough of my friends?
  Do I get enough exercise?
  What am I eating?
  Most of all, when am I going to stop thinking *me* and
    start thinking of *you*?

Defuse me, Lord,

with your soothing grace,
your quiet caring,
your ease, and rest
in you.   Amen.

THANKSGIVING

Thank you Father for so many things I take for granted,
especially the gift of each new day. Help me to
understand that your gift of life is not just for me, and
that I am created to be part of others, and therefore able
to feel the importance of being most of all close to you.

Let us thank God silently, each of us, for some of the
beautiful things that have come into our ordinary lives.

Neither in clouds above our sight,
Nor in far time above our ken
Nor in the darkness of the night,
Nor in rare moments now and then
But at this instant on this spot
By hearth and heath in old and new
The common kind of thing is what
I see God's glory streaming through.

John Clare 1793–1864

This is the Lord's doing:
and it is marvellous in our eyes.
This is the day which the Lord has made:
we will rejoice and be glad in it.   *Psalm 118:23–24*

If our mouths were full of song as the sea,
our tongues with joyful sounds like the roar of its
    waves,
our lips with praise as the outspread sky
our eyes shining like the sun and the moon
our hands stretched out like eagles' wings in the air,
our feet as swift as the wild deer;
we still could not thank you enough, Lord.

Sabbath Morning Prayer, Forms of Prayer for Jewish Worship

Father of all, we give you thanks and praise, that when
we were still far off you met us in your son and
brought us home. Dying and living, he declared your
love, gave us grace, and opened the gate of glory. May
we who share Christ's body live his risen life; we who
drink his cup bring life to others; we whom the spirit
lights give light to the world. Keep us in this hope that
we have grasped, so that we and all your children shall
be free, and the whole earth live to praise your name;
through Jesus Christ our Lord.   Amen.

Series 3 Communion Rite

TIME

Time heals. *Anonymous*

Time is nature's way of stopping everything happening
at once. *Anonymous*

Be swift to love! Make haste to be kind.
Henri Frédéric Amiel 1828–1881

Remember, then, there is only one time that is
important, *now*. *Leo Tolstoy 1828–1910*

Time past and time future
What might have been and what has been
Point to one end, which is always present.
T. S. Eliot 1888–1965, 'Burnt Norton'

Lord, when I am torn by time, by rushing and
worrying about myself or others; when I am wearied
and pained or cause pain to others; when I am noisy
and thoughtless, or self-indulgent or rude; when I am
thoughtless and careless, not listening for your voice,
then Lord, in your great love, your great
understanding, and your great peace, give me true time
and proper rest, to be blessed by your calm and healed
in my soul, through Jesus Christ our Lord.   Amen.

TIREDNESS

Lord teach me to listen to my body, to know when to rest.

Lord grant me rest in you. Give me in your most loving care, ease from burdens, strengthened trust, and tranquillity of mind, that from the calm of sleep I may awake refreshed with joy at the gift of a new day.   Amen.

TOLERANCE

Culture is a word that describes the state of a man's mind; not the contents of a mind but attitudes of mind. *Interest, zest, curiosity, tolerance.*

Harold Nicolson 1886–1968

TOUCHING

Lord help me to remember that touching reverently and lovingly in your name is an important reassurance to others.

Help me to remember that it is almost impossible to be angry with someone you touch frequently.

TOWERBLOCK (tyranny)

Noise that is to the right, left, above and below;
cutting the telephone wire;
hand through the door;
lifts that are fouled;
cars vandalised;
child immigrant suicide;
charming, Lord, charming.

TRAGEDY

There can be no Christian tragedy because Christianity always implies the possibility of reconciliation and atonement. The apparent end of human life is not the real end.   *George Steiner*

TREASURES

I have three treasures;
Guard them and keep them safe:
The first is love,
The second is, Never too much,
The third is, Never be the first in the world.

Through love, one has no fear;
Through not doing too much, one has amplitude
  (of reserve power);
Through not presuming to be the first in the world,
  one can develop one's talent and let it mature.

For love is victorious in attack,
  and invulnerable in defence.
Heaven arms with love
  those it would not see destroyed.

Lao Tze 604BC

TREES

I think that I shall never see
A poem as lovely as a tree.

A tree whose hungry mouth is pressed
Against the sweet earth's flowing breast;

A tree that looks at God all day
And lifts her leafy arms to pray;

A tree that may in summer wear
A nest of robins in her hair;

Upon whose bosom snow has lain;
Who intimately lives with rain.

Poems are made by fools like me,
But only God can make a tree.

Alfred Joyce Kilmer 1886–1918

TROUBLE

Come to me, all you who are weary and heavy laden,
and I will give you rest. Take my yoke upon you and
learn from me; for I am gentle and humble of heart and

you shall find rest for your souls. For my yoke is easy
and my burden is light.

Matthew 11:28, tr. Dorothy L. Sayers 1893–1957

TRUST

In thee O Lord I have trusted;
Let me never be confounded.

Te Deum

I will say unto the Lord, thou art my hope and my
   stronghold:
My God, in him I will trust.

Psalm 91:2

Fear nothing, for I am with you, be not afraid, for I am
your God.

Isaiah 41:10

One night a man had a dream. He dreamed he was
walking along a beach with our Lord. Across the sky
flashed scenes from his life. For each scene he noticed
two sets of footprints in the sand; one belonging to
him, and the other to the Lord.

When the last scene of his life flashed before him, he
looked back at the footprints in the sand. He noticed
that many times along the path of his life there was
only the one set of footprints, and at the very lowest
and saddest times in his life.

This really bothered him and he questioned our Lord
about it. 'Lord, you said that once I decided to follow
you, you'd walk with me all the way. But I have
noticed that during the most troublesome times in my
life, there is only one set of footprints. I don't
understand why when I needed you most you would
leave me.'

Our Lord replied, 'You know that I love you and
would never leave you. During your times of trial and
suffering, when you see only one set of footprints, it
was then that I carried you.'   *Anonymous*

That you are Lord to me
suffices me for strength;
that I am servant to you
suffices for my glory.   *Arabic prayer*

It was Tubby Clayton, the founder of Toc H, who used
to say, 'You win men by trusting them.'

Many of us have such bad memories because we do not
trust them.   *Reg Bazire*

Trust the man who hesitates in his speech and is quick
and ready in action, but beware of long arguments and
long beards.

George Santayana 1863–1919

TRUTH

Truth is a relationship.   *Anonymous*

Of course the truth hurts. You would too, if you got
kicked around so much.   *Franklin P. Jones*

Prefer the truth and right by which you seem to lose,
to the falsehood and wrong by which you seem to gain.
Moses Maimonides 1135–1204

Lord, cast out from me whatsoever loves to make a lie,
and bring me into the perfect freedom of your
truth.   Amen.

Bishop Brooke Foss Westcott 1825–1901 (adapted)

UNCERTAINTY

Man must learn to bear a certain portion of uncertainty.
Sigmund Freud 1856–1939

UNDERSTANDING

The darkness is no darkness with thee.

Psalm 139:12

Thou requirest truth in the inward parts;
And thou shalt make me to understand wisdom
  secretly.

Psalm 51:6

To understand all is to forgive all.
Madame de Staël 1766–1817

And the peace of God which surpasses all
understanding, keep your heart and mind in the
knowledge and love of God.

Philippians 4:7

UNITY

Unity is strength.

UNIVERSALITY

Much have I seen and known; cities of men
And manners, climates, councils, governments . . .
I am part of all that I have met.

Alfred, Lord Tennyson 1809–1892

UNSELFISHNESS

. . . the more I give to thee the more I have
For both are infinite.

William Shakespeare 1564–1616, Romeo and Juliet

I sought my soul
  And the soul I could not see
I sought my God
  And God eluded me
I sought my brother
  And found all three.

Anonymous

Unselfishness at home enables Christ to enter.

It is when the 'I' in our lives is big and God is small
that unhappiness spreads.

It is when God in our lives is big and I is small that, in and through service to others, we find peace, fulfilment and joy.   Amen.
See also Selflessness

USEFULNESS

Store what you must;
Share what you can.

All men know the advantages of being useful, but no one knows the advantage of being useless.

Khieh-Yu

VIGILANCE

Civilisation cannot ever be taken for granted. Its price is eternal vigilance and ceaseless spiritual effort.

Edmund Burke 1729–1797

VIOLENCE

For the uncontrolled there is no wisdom, and without concentration there is no peace.   *The Bhagavadgita*

To be violent is to be weak. Violence has no mind. Is it not wiser to seek a man's love than to desire his swift defeat?   *Chinese aphorism*

A gun is an instrument which can fulfil its purpose only through destruction. As sound injures the ear, so its discharge consumes the flesh.   *Chinese aphorism*

VISITING

Help me Lord not to be loud, incessant, talkative, and insensitive. Give me the courage to be still and to offer the healing gift of silence.
   Help me to match the present need, through Jesus Christ our Lord.   Amen.

The quiet holding of a hand is often enough. Thank you Lord.

The friend

Here he comes, fresh, clean, bright and brimming with life. A good friend, a reliable friend, but I don't think I can take all that vitality. Not here in this hospital bed. Not today with this pain and discomfort, in spite of thoughtful doctors and kind nurses. Ah, Lord, please, under no circumstances let him make me laugh. I just can't take laughter. Oh how I dread this.

Nearer and nearer, and here. 'Hello', he says, and instead of brisk chatter, he reads my eyes, and says little more except, 'How do you feel?' 'The headache's terrible,' I reply. 'Then why not transfer the pressure and hold my hand.' We clasp, as if shaking hands, and without a word he grips my hand for an hour and a half. Then, I feel very tired, and he blesses me. Thanks Dad. Thanks for being a true friend. For saying little and then nothing. Thanks for letting me know God's presence in your hand and your silence . . . But then you *are* a true friend. Thanks.

(The patient sleeps and the priest moves on.)

WAITING

    Now I'm waiting;
    and waiting always kills.

    But it also cures
      and saves
        and heals.

    Lord, I am content
    to wait . . .

    O Lord I am just waiting
    Waiting for the moving of the waters —
    Waiting for your hand to move and point
    In the direction you want me to go.
    Lord I have tried — tried so hard
      to plan the next move,

And somewhere inside me Lord I'm still trying.
And yet Lord my life is as clay in the
    hands of the potter.
I cannot make myself, I cannot use myself,
I can but wait and if you want — go on waiting
    knowing that —
You can take even this deeply marred vessel
    and use it,
Fashioning it continually for the purpose —
    you have for it.
O Lord give me patience, and humility
    and vitality.
Help me to be content, dear Lord,
    to wait and rest on you
For this speck of time is eternity.

Author unknown

Each day was like a year whose days are long.
    Oscar Wilde 1854–1900, 'The Ballad of Reading Gaol'

As the seashell contains the sand of ocean
As the sun gives life to the universe
And the moon gives hope through another light,
Help me to contain the power of your love
within my waiting, and to know
that such power is for me
a well very deep
filled by the waters
of real life,
life with you, here.

WARNING

If we would avoid fear — we must feed love;
If we would avoid arrogance — we must feed need;
If we would avoid betrayal — we must feed
    compassion;
If we would avoid pride — we must feed reality.

WASHING

Create in me a clean heart.   *Psalm 51:10*

Who can bring a clean thing out of an unclean?

Job 14:4

Wash me thoroughly.

Psalm 51:2

There are those who are pure in their own eyes but are
not cleansed.   *Proverbs 30:12*

How long will it be before you are made clean?

Jeremiah 13:27

Wash yourselves — make yourselves clean.

Isaiah 1:16

Blessed are the pure in heart.

Matthew 5:8

WEAKNESS

What ought to make us most afraid is our weakness,
our cowardice, our detestable nature; but we escape
this fear precisely by casting ourselves on our Lord,
relying on him to save us, in spite of everything.

Abbé de Tourville

To rely on others is to be uneasy.

Buddhist scripture

Thought shall be keener,
heart the harder,
courage the greater,
as our might lessens.

Anglo-Saxon, c. 1000AD

WEARINESS

Art thou weary,
art thou laden,
art thou sore distrest?
Come to me, saith one
and coming
be at rest.

J.M. Neale 1816–1866

WEATHER
Rain (anticipating)

Dear Lord, you came in the season of winds and rains
to be born a child, to herald the light of gentle love and
tenderness. In this often harsh and insensitive world
come into my life with the fulness of your caring.

Show me how to include others in my life, that in
loving and caring for them I may know the warming
gift of your presence.   Amen.

Snow (revealing)

Child of the snow
Peaceful as heaven
Warm as love
Gift of my life, Lord Jesus
Friend of my life, Lord Jesus
Hear my prayer.

Child of the light
Gentle as silence
Calm as peace
Strengthen me now, Lord Jesus
Befriend me now, Lord Jesus
Hear my prayer.

Wind (empowering)

God of the summer air, free as a flame, strong as the
wind, show me your beauty enfolding us all. Let me
see your glory and feel your love as they embrace every
aspect of life: our factories and shops; our hospitals

and homes; our shipyards and rivers; our prisons and schools; our city streets and country lanes.

Kindle this area (town, village etc), this people, this land with the glow of your faith, the flame of your hope, and the fire of your love, that in being grateful for what has been, and joyous for what we can give, we may be purposed to live every day in the power of your Holy Spirit, through Jesus Christ our Lord. Amen.

WELCOME

Say little and do much, and receive all men with a cheerful countenance.   *Talmud*

Welcome to my home, come in with love,
With love I hope you'll stay
Accepting me for what I am
In no material way.   *Moira A. Nicholls*

WISDOM

The hours of folly are measured by the clock;
but of wisdom, no clock can measure.
William Blake 1757–1827

If one has to praise someone do it by word of mouth rather that writing. And if to be castigated, also by word of mouth.   *Chang Ch'Ao 1676*

In the midst of great joy do not promise to give a man everything.

In the midst of great anger do not answer a man's letter.   *Chinese*

When wisdom comes into your heart and knowledge is a pleasure to you, discretion will watch over you and reason will guard you.
Proverbs 2:10-11, Forms of Prayer for Jewish Worship

A wise man does not speak before someone greater
  than himself in wisdom.
He does not cut into his fellow's speech.
He does not rush to reply.
He asks what is relevant and answers to the point.
He speaks about first things first, and about last things
  last.
As to what he has not heard he says, 'I did not hear it.'
He acknowledges the truth.
The reverse of all these applies to the uncultured man.
Sayings of the Fathers, Forms of Prayer for Jewish Worship

On the bookshelf of life, God is a useful work of
reference always at hand but seldom consulted.

Dag Hammarskjöld 1905–1961

To reach perfection, we must all pass, one by one,
through the death of self-effacement.

Dag Hammarskjöld 1905–1961

Do not look for every quality in one individual.

Shoo King

WONDER
   Lord let me never lose my sense of wonder, and ever
   deepen my appreciation of life.   Amen.

WORLDLINESS
   People who care over-much for the works of man end
   by losing all sense of the works of God. And even their
   friends become mere pieces of decoration.

Harold Nicolson 1886–1968

WORRY

Lord I worry about . . . people with two mortgages, monthly payments on the TV, car and household goods. I wonder who suffers most.

Is it the wife and mother, with the extra job, Dad rushing headlong into a coronary, or the children, missing love and companionship?

Help us all, Lord, to pause and plan, to find real values in family life, rather than material things that pass away. Amen.
Roger Bush

WORSHIP

This day for Israel is light and is joy, a Sabbath of rest.
Sabbath Evening Service, Forms of Prayer for Jewish Worship

If you do not worship you'll shrink; it's as brutal as that.
Peter Shaffer b. 1926, Equus

YEAR, A new

Bless this year, O Lord our God, and may all that it brings be good for us. Blessed are you Lord, who blesses the years.
Daily Amidah, Forms of Prayer for Jewish Worship

The old year has died, and the new year has scarcely begun. In this pause before the account is made of the past, and my life is judged for what it is, I ask for honesty, vision and courage. Honesty to see myself as I am, vision to see myself as I should be, and the courage to change and realise myself.
Forms of Prayer for Jewish Worship

Index